Literacy Beyond the Classroom

Literacy Beyond the Classroom

Ten real-world projects proven to raise attainment in primary English

**Dominic Traynor and
Cath Bufton-Green**

BLOOMSBURY EDUCATION

LONDON OXFORD NEW YORK NEW DELHI SYDNEY

BLOOMSBURY EDUCATION
Bloomsbury Publishing Plc
50 Bedford Square, London, WC1B 3DP, UK

BLOOMSBURY, BLOOMSBURY EDUCATION and the Diana logo are
trademarks of Bloomsbury Publishing Plc

First published in Great Britain, 2020

A catalogue record for this book is available from the British Library

ISBN: PB: 978-1-4729-6803-6; ePDF: 978-1-4729-6802-9; ePub: 978-1-4729-6801-2

2 4 6 8 10 9 7 5 3 1 (paperback)

Typeset by Newgen KnowledgeWorks Pvt. Ltd., Chennai, India
Printed and bound by CPI Group (UK) Ltd, Croydon, CR0 4YY

To find out more about our authors and books visit www.bloomsbury.com
and sign up for our newsletters

Contents

Foreword

'Creativity is as important now in education as literacy and we should treat it with the same status.' Sir Ken Robinson

We've all heard it. Creativity, creative problem-solving, creative thinking, creative literacy… By now, every educator knows that these are critical skills that every child must develop. Indeed, there is overwhelming evidence that creativity in the classroom impacts both short-term success in improved education outcomes, as well as longer-term success in the workforce. On the other hand, if we fail to nurture our pupils' innate creativity, we are doing them a disservice, effectively robbing them of their future. This is why innovative educators are constantly seeking new ways to inject creativity into their classrooms.

Understanding the importance of nurturing and encouraging creativity is the easy part. Knowing how this translates into classroom activities is trickier.

Tools are obviously important. This is why Adobe created Spark, an easy-to-use creation tool that is available for free to pupils of all ages. Spark was designed to be fun, approachable and readily available. To this end, Spark works on just about any device you have in the classroom. It runs in the web browser on all desktop computers, and has been optimised to run on Chromebooks. Adobe Spark was built to fundamentally shift how your pupils interact with content, allowing them to focus on what they want to share rather than how to do so. The tool is designed to be engaging and encouraging, while getting out of the way so as to let pupil creativity flourish.

But great tools are not enough. And so the best educators turn to their peers, fellow educators, to learn from them. It's why I co-authored my own book on injecting creativity into the classroom. And it's why Adobe created the Education Exchange, a community of close to a million educators who question, discuss, collaborate, share and inspire.

My colleague Dominic Traynor is an accomplished educator in his own right. His work at LitFilmFest has helped thousands of pupils find their passions and voices, allowing them to create and share with the world. And more recently, as part of the Adobe Education team, he's been helping lead the effort in guiding educators to understand the role of creativity in the classroom and how to encourage it.

I'm therefore excited to see that he has taken this hard-earned experience and condensed it into a format easily shared with all. *Literacy Beyond the Classroom* includes ready-to-use projects all built using Adobe Spark. In addition, he has included interviews with leaders in education and industry to provide guidance and insight into how to best equip our pupils for success in the future. As an educator, I am fortunate to have been granted early access to parts of this book. I eagerly await reading the rest, as I know you will too.

Ben Forta
Educator, author and Senior Director of Education Initiatives,
Adobe Systems Incorporated

Introduction

In 1984, the Irish government was worried it wouldn't be able to enforce a ban on smoking in classrooms. Really. A 1984 briefing memo for the Taoiseach's department read:

> 'Smoking is not forbidden for teachers while they are on duty but it is not encouraged, and teachers are expected to refrain from smoking in the classroom. However, in some schools, smoking in the classroom is an accepted practice.
>
> The Minister feels that a ban would have great exemplary value and would encounter little opposition from responsible parents, teachers or pupils. While there may be difficulty in imposing it, the minster feels that the ban on smoking should be absolute and apply to teachers as well as pupils.'

It seems absolutely mad to think that this was the situation in the mid-eighties, but go back just a generation or two and you're in an alternative universe where smoking is promoted by doctors and dentists, as a way to pick up women and even to be an athlete! It wasn't until 1998 that all British Airways flights were smoke-free and it was only 13 years ago that you could still smoke in pubs and restaurants. Imagine trying to smoke in a classroom, a restaurant or a plane now. People would go crazy. Through education and legislation, radical change on a mass scale is possible.

Effecting change through education

I have an enormous passion for the role that education plays in effecting change. Both my parents were primary school teachers and I promised myself that I would never be a teacher, having seen the amount of work that my mum did after the school day had long finished. But obviously two weeks at Christmas and a long summer holiday were just too good to ignore and I ended up becoming a primary school teacher myself…

In truth, it wasn't about the holidays at all. After trying other jobs, I wanted a career that gave me the most direct route to making the world a better place. I've asked thousands of teachers why they became teachers and the most common answer by a country mile is that they want to make a difference; they want to improve the lives of children because children give us the chance to make a better world.

I love teaching and it's given me my proudest moments but, let's be honest, teachers are exhausted. There's precious little opportunity for us to talk about whether the things we're teaching are actually making the world a better place. This is a huge problem for our society. I believe our children are sleepwalking into a future that will be very different from the one we want them to inherit.

For example, we're currently on track by 2050 to give our children a world that has more plastic in the sea than fish. CNN have reported that The Great Pacific Garbage Patch, a huge collection of litter in the North Pacific Ocean, is now three times the size of France. LADbible recently applied to the United Nations to get this area officially recognised as a country called The Trash Isles, complete with passport and currency. Rumour has it that Ryanair are already selling flights.

Food waste is another issue facing our children. Between 33 and 50 per cent of all food produced globally is never eaten and yet it is estimated that one in five children in the UK are what's called food insecure, lacking secure access to sufficient, healthy food. A major consequence of food waste is that our soil is 30 to 40 years away from soil infertility, all to produce food that we then just throw away. And how about child obesity? Right now, one in five kids leave primary school obese. This health crisis is matched by the country's mental health crisis too – one in five children will experience a mental health difficulty at least once during their first 11 years of life.

Plastic pollution, food waste, obesity and mental health, just a few issues our children will face and we aren't being encouraged to teach them the information and skills to deal with them. Instead, we're put under pressure to teach to tests that don't prepare children for the present, never mind the future.

So, it's all pretty bleak. But despite all of this, you might be surprised to hear that I am overwhelmingly optimistic, for the very reason that I've seen what happens when we give power to our pupils.

Pupil power

Have you noticed how we don't ever think of our adult leaders as having been children? We can't imagine that they would have sung Kumbaya in assembly or played with their friends in the school playground. But children in classrooms everywhere are growing up to become our leaders, the drivers of industry, and the most powerful force of all, our adult consumers. Rather than us leaving blinkers on our children so they sleepwalk into a bleak future, we can start teaching the content, values and skills that create a world in which our children don't just survive but thrive.

Between the ages of five and 16, every child spends the majority of their waking life in school. We have the opportunity to get the next generation tackling our greatest challenges from an early age so that, by the time they become adults, they will consider things like plastic, food waste or junk food as crazy as smoking on a plane, in a classroom or in a restaurant would be to us now.

Let's make innovators like scientists and social entrepreneurs the new celebrities in the eyes of our children. Plastic bottles are one of the worst contributors to plastic pollution yet we have innovators and entrepreneurs making edible water capsules from seaweed and even clothing and footwear from plastic litter. Food waste? TooGoodToGo allows you to buy unsold food at knockdown prices from top eateries to prevent it from being thrown away. The OLIO food app makes it simple for people to give surplus food to others in their community. SNACT makes fruit snacks from ugly fruit in compostable packaging. Why not use our classrooms to promote these innovators?

Let's teach children to understand politics so they vote for positive change and hold politicians to account, and so people of all backgrounds become politicians themselves. By developing a sophisticated electorate, we can make sure we get the progressive politics that we need for the benefit of our society as a whole.

Let's develop a generation of sophisticated consumers who control industry by reading about sustainable companies, by writing news reports and adverts about them. Why not deliver a curriculum that creates responsible consumers?

And let's improve mental health by reading and writing about mental health and bringing daily mindfulness sessions into the classroom.

Where does literacy come into all this?

Now, maybe you think this is all well and good but we can't waste time on this hippy nonsense when we need academic results in the classroom. As part of the EDUCATE programme from the UCL Institute of Education, the world leader in education research, I was part of a team who designed a range of projects that followed the National Curriculum for English and engaged primary pupils aged seven to 11 with a mix of fiction, politics, health, creativity, sustainability and digital skills. Their traditional English skills improved by 3.75 times the national average rate. In other words, they made 15 months' progress in just four months. And if this all now sounds *too* serious, and you think we should just let kids be kids and let them have fun, I'm pleased to tell you the research showed that there was also a 50 per cent increase in levels of enjoyment in English learning. As Einstein said, 'That is the way to learn the most; when you are doing something with such enjoyment that you don't notice that the time passes.'

One of the projects we designed had a class of nine- to ten-year-olds improving their persuasive writing by starting a change.org petition to ban plastic straws in the UK. It had over 100,000 signatures. The children were interviewed like celebrities on BBC Radio, featured in the *Metro* and on CNN, and congratulated in Parliament. We also had classes improving their news reporting and political speech-writing skills. This class interviewed the Welsh Minister for Education about how their current curriculum does not give them the skills they need for their future. They investigated how politics works, held their representatives accountable, wrote news stories and delivered political speeches.

It's so crucial to take the kids' enthusiasm for projects like this and make them feel celebrated for the work that they've done. As we continued to develop our approach to teaching English through these real-world projects and shared this with schools across the country, we decided to go one step further and develop a festival called LitFilmFest. It started in 2014 and has seen well over a million six- to 14-year-olds take part. We ask the children to complete projects as part of the festival and we then get their work featured on the YouTube Kids app, endorsed by BBC Good Food, Parliament UK and former children's laureate Michael Rosen and seen on big screens around the country, whether that's in a school hall or at the IMAX in Waterloo, the biggest cinema screen in Britain.

In this book, I am excited to share, with the help of former preparatory school headteacher and educational consultant, Cath Bufton-Green, the LitFilmFest approach, so you can use it in your classroom too. In these pages, you will find ten projects that you can complete with primary pupils. Each project aims to help children learn about a global challenge the world is currently facing while simultaneously developing the literacy skills required by the National Curriculum for English. There are also opportunities to go even further and create videos to bring all your pupils' hard work to life! I hope the projects will bring literacy to life in your classroom, so children enjoy reading and writing and see its relevance in the world around them, while also helping you to develop well-rounded, responsible global citizens.

What will I find in each chapter?

Beginning with an **introduction**, each chapter provides you with some background to the global challenge being tackled. Packed with statistics, the introduction will give you the key information you need to teach the topic. This information doesn't necessarily need to be shared with the children, but we have flagged the key information you should share to help introduce the topic to the class. Look out for the **share with the class** boxes. You can, of course, share additional information from the introduction if appropriate. This will depend on the age and level of the children and where your discussions take you during the course of the lessons. You should also look out for the **talking points** we have suggested. These are simple questions you can raise with the class as you introduce the topic to help engage children and get them thinking about the key issues.

Following the introduction, we've included an **interview** with someone who is a leading expert on the chapter topic. From Natasha Devon discussing mental health to Michael Rosen talking about education, we hope these interviews will give you a fascinating and thought-provoking insight into the topic. There is also an **Atlas of the Future case study** in each chapter to provide an inspiring and engaging real-life example of companies, organisations and individuals making a difference. The case studies are included by kind permission of Atlas of the Future, a non-profit organisation that aims to raise the profile of people and projects working to create a better world. The case studies will show you what humans are capable of when it comes to tackling global issues and I hope they will inspire you to see what your class can achieve too. If appropriate for the level your children are working at, you can share these interviews and case studies (or extracts from them) with your class before getting started on the project work. They can be a great way into the topic.

Next, you will find a **project** to complete with your class over the course of five or six lessons. The projects are designed to fit in with whatever way you usually structure your learning experiences, so they can be run on consecutive days over the course of a week, for example, or you could spread them over a series of weeks. Where possible, we recommend teaching them on consecutive days to gather momentum. A clear plan is provided for each lesson, split into an introduction, a main session and a plenary, and complete with timings and full instructions for each activity. Throughout the project, there are **teaching tips** to give you helpful guidance on running the lessons, as well as **examples** of the type of work you can expect children to produce. Accompanying some of the lesson plans are **online resources**, which you will need to run the sessions. These resources include example videos of the projects in action. Please do take a look at these videos to inspire your teaching and to see what your own class can achieve. There are also additional interviews available online, providing further insights into the challenges the book discusses and education more generally. You can find all resources at **www.bloomsbury.com/ literacy-beyond-the-classroom**. The project in Chapter 10: STEM to STEAM takes a slightly different format, as it's a project that's best completed over the course of a single day. Why not make it really memorable and run it as an exciting special event during British Science Week?

Many of the projects in this book involve creating short videos to bring your pupils' work to life. **Adobe Spark Video** is the perfect tool for this and I highly recommend using it for editing your videos in the classroom. It is free to download from the App Store and can be used intuitively by staff and pupils to quickly create effective videos to share. You may also want to use **Adobe Rush**, a more advanced editing tool that comes with three free exports when you sign up. A mobile app is also available. You can find tutorial videos on getting started with Adobe Spark and Adobe Rush in the online resources.

*

If we want to create a healthy future generation full of rock star scientists like Brian Cox, activists like Maya Angelou, innovators like James Dyson and guardians of the planet like Ellen MacArthur, let's show our children that we value these efforts more than appearing on *Big Brother*.

Teachers have always appreciated how important it is for children to read as much as possible. As well as fiction, let's give equal importance to reading and writing about innovation, citizenship, sustainability and health. A child who reads fiction can dream of a better life. A child who reads non-fiction and learns about reality has the power to make dreams come true. I want kids to read *Stig of the Dump*, but also study how the rubbish in Stig's dump got there and what they can do about it. I want kids to read *Matilda* and then read about Malala, learning how young girls can bring about big changes. And I want kids to read *War Game*, understand that bad things can happen when diplomacy fails and see healthy political debate as part of their everyday lives.

Children give us the chance to make a better world. I don't want to let kids be just kids because I know that's not good enough for them. I want to give power to our pupils so they feel like superheroes. I want them to grow into adults and make this the kind of world we all want it to be for generations of children to come.

Dominic Traynor

Chapter 1
Pupil politics

Introduction

It is a time-honoured tradition for older generations to accuse younger generations of political apathy. Today, however, proponents of the 'young people don't care about politics' rhetoric have statistics on their side – statistics which reveal an alarmingly low turnout of young people in national elections.

But does refusing to vote indeed signal political apathy amongst the youth? Or is there another emerging trend of pupil politics which favours activism and direct confrontation over casting a ballot? And is this new way of being a young political citizen more impactful in the long run or more damaging to a stable society?

In this chapter...

In this chapter we will explore these topics and present the important role that schools play in getting pupils engaged with politics at an early age and motivating them to become an active voter at 18. There is an insightful interview with global thought leader David Price, and a case study from America about an organisation called 'Eighteen × 18': a creative platform set up to engage the younger generation to get active and vote. These can be shared with your class before getting started on the Pupil Prime Minister project. In this ten-lesson project your pupils will begin to understand the landscape of government, learn the semantics of politics, including the use of persuasive language and evidence to support their beliefs, and create their own mini-manifesto.

Why young people don't vote

Voting is considered the cornerstone of democracy. If people don't show up to vote, the system doesn't work – large swathes of society quite simply find themselves underrepresented. Statistics show that this is exactly what is happening with the youth of today.

Out of a total of 61 per cent voter turnout in 2005, young voters amounted to just 36 per cent. In 2010, that figure rose slightly to 43 per cent out of a total of 65 per cent voter turnout. More tellingly though, despite an overall voter increase to 78 per cent in the 2017 general election, young voter figures remained static, at just 43 per cent.

What these figures indicate is that the narrative of a youth turnout surge is, to all intents and purposes, factually inaccurate. And yet, when we delve deeper into things, we see that this does not mean that young people are apolitical, but rather that they are jaded with a political system they feel alienated from.

Young people don't turn out to vote for varied and complicated reasons, but at a fundamental level, it all boils down to trust. Or rather, the lack of it.

When we think about the processes we teach and promote in schools, we are encouraging our pupils to have a voice and be proud of their opinions, no matter if they differ from others. We provide opportunities for structured debate and transparent discussion, for supporting arguments and for openly admitting when we are wrong. Is it any wonder then, that our young people look at our current world of politics with scepticism, when they see those in charge falling short on these qualities?

What is conceived as 'apathy' today stems from a decline in trust in both the decision-makers who hold key positions of power and the system in general. This decline in trust is not unfounded. In the last decade alone, an array of scandals have exposed corruption on multiple levels: from corporations to elected officials, from media moguls to whole governments.

Scandals, like MP expenses in 2009, WikiLeaks in 2010, phone-hacking in 2011, the Panama Papers of 2015 and the seemingly daily scandals from the White House involving Donald Trump, imply that truth can only be found by unearthing hidden data and that governments are inherently deceitful. This distrust towards politicians and governments has also extended to distrust in traditional media, who are perceived as mouthpieces of a controlled political agenda, and therefore part of the problem.

So, why bother voting, if it means being part of a process that is rigged from the start? Young people leaving school and reaching voting age have predominantly been used to honest and transparent voting systems in school that lead to outcomes that are true to the swell of interest. They have seen those in charge pay homage to the results and pupil voice, and make changes based on what the voters believe in and need. They see integrity in those with power and build trust in the systems provided for decision-making and development.

However, entering the real world of political systems, and seeing the way it operates and undermines their beliefs, leads them towards a conscious refuting of democracy in its traditional form and to finding alternative ways to have their views represented. According to a survey of British Social Attitudes in 2010, despite there being low trust in politicians, the interest in politics had risen. This brings us to the heart of the issue and the key to understanding a new phenomenon: that of pupil politics.

How the youth of today is shaping the political landscape

It makes sense that, by not turning up to vote, young people of today would be underrepresented in government. Although that particular tide seems to be turning in the US and Canada, in Europe the percentage of parliamentarians under 30 still remains at an abysmal 0.5 per cent.

Share with the class

Considering that Generation Z or Gen Z (anyone born after 1996) now accounts for 32 per cent of the world's population, surpassing even millennials (anyone born between 1980 and 1996), one would think that the political system would do a better job in trying to engage them. Political parties are, for the most part, not only comprised of older people, but also thought of as an 'older people construct'. When asked the likelihood of becoming candidates in future elections, only 14.5 per cent of EU youngsters said yes. And yet, this generation is very much interested and invested in politics – low voting turnout notwithstanding. They're just going about it in a different way.

The politically active youngsters of today are focusing their attention on activism, becoming spokespeople for societal change. They care less about being connected to a political party, opting instead to start and support grassroots movements. It seems, therefore, that pupil politics has transcended political party lines.

Share with the class

A great example of pupil politics comes from the US in the wake of the Parkland, Florida school shooting tragedy. The high-school students who survived the massacre organised marches on a wide scale to raise awareness of gun violence issues; their message quickly became viral online, giving them a global platform. This has, in turn, given them the power to pressurise politicians. Some Republican governors and senators are now starting to

> support background checks prior to gun purchasing thanks to this wave of pressure, and companies are beginning to withdraw their support of the NRA (the American National Rifle Association).

Pushing for change in such a vocal and viral way is considered an immature approach to politics by some. The thinking goes that there is simply a way that things must be done, and this isn't it. However, the belief that 'older people know better' is being challenged every day.

During her talk at the Royal Festival Hall in London, Michelle Obama didn't hesitate to share with her audience that, in her experience, the people who run the world are simply not that smart.

She noted, 'There's a lot of things that folks are doing to keep their seats because they don't want to share power. And what better way to do it than to make you think you don't belong? If you think about it in these terms, perhaps it is imperative that young people join the political discourse in their own, irreverent way.'

In light of this, it is very difficult to maintain this idea of an 'apathetic' youth suggested by the low turnout of young voters in elections. Pupil politics of today are making it very clear that voting is not the only way to express one's engagement in social issues. If anything, grassroots campaigning, online petitions and 'calling out' politicians may actually be more efficient ways of interacting in today's politics than showing up to vote.

Voting may still be considered the cornerstone of democracy, but young people are proving that a different architecture for democracy itself is not only possible, but perhaps necessary.

Young people might be bypassing the ballot box more than we'd like and this is something we need to influence, but they are still intent on changing the world. Imagine what might happen if we could encourage them to do both.

Interview with David Price

Introducing…

David Price OBE is a global thought leader, learning futurist and author, specialising in how organisations learn, innovate and make themselves fit for the future. He is a highly sought-after public speaker, entertaining and educating audiences around the world, in business, education and the public sector. His most recent book, *OPEN: How We'll Work, Live and Learn in The Future*, has been an Amazon bestseller since its publication.

To what extent do you think that young people should take part in the current political system or bypass it?

If I was a young person, I would be thinking, 'Why do I want to get involved in this?' But on the other hand, it's the system we've got and will you have any kind of influence if you just bypass the system? That's why I love the Parklands kids and Greta Thunberg because they give a lie to this myth of Generation Z not being interested in world affairs. This is the most morally and ethically engaged generation there's ever been. They're passionate about it and frustrated that the system doesn't allow for their ideas to flourish.

Should politics be part of the curriculum? Absolutely, but it should be way more radical, to explore values and attitudes. We're at a point where we cannot take moral and ethical considerations out of the curriculum. It's not about brainwashing kids to have a certain viewpoint. It's about encouraging them to think for themselves at a time when the climate is suffering, and cultural understanding and politics are in a mess. It's not about making them have one particular stance; it's about them defining their own stance, being able to defend that stance and being able to accept opinions that are different from their own.

We're living in a country where it's all about who shouts loudest and no one's listening to each other. If education tries to pretend that that's for someone else to get involved in, what kind of future are we preparing our children for? How do we expect children to improve the system if we don't talk about it in the classroom? So, when we've got young people who are standing up for what they believe in, like the climate strikers, we should be nurturing them, valuing them and giving them an education that enables them to do all of that effectively, but instead, they are criticised for bunking off one day of school. What a load of nonsense.

What do you make of the current education system's approach to preparing young people for the future?

I look at students in international schools and it really hits me just how much better prepared they are than the average school in the UK. It's not just about more arts and sports provision, it's about them doing the International Baccalaureate, a second or third language, real-life experiences with employers, and so on. They have the freedom to try things and open their minds to things that the average UK state school student will never get to experience. I think that's about mindset more than money.

In the UK, if the only yardstick we approach the success of an intervention with is how well they perform in short-term memory tests, then we'll forever be off track and having the wrong conversation. Of course, those children will do well because they're being drilled to pass tests but will that help them in 20 years' time?

Around 40 per cent of workers are freelancers and yet that hasn't affected how we teach children. I say to teachers, just imagine that 40 per cent of your kids will never get a traditional career. What would you teach them? They say things like creativity, resilience and how to market themselves. So why don't we? Why do they have to wait until they find that they're never going to get a proper job before they learn those skills? What I'm saying is that the future is right now and freelancing is going to be something they're forced into with all the benefits and negatives that it brings. So, let's get them tooled up to deal with it. How come the curriculum in the majority of schools isn't reflecting that reality? The same ten subjects that were around in the 1840s are the same ones that we teach today.

The difference between pupils in schools using project-based learning and developing communication skills and the pupils in your average school is so significant. They are completely comfortable with presenting and talking to adults, something that employers are constantly complaining about when taking on young people. We've known this stuff for 15 years yet it's not showing up in our curriculum approach. Young people are communicating to each other using their thumbs on their phones so how can we be surprised if they can't communicate in person or in front of a group if we aren't giving them the chance to do it? To me, this is one of the urgent things that we've got to do: define what we mean by a future-facing curriculum.

How would you approach designing a new curriculum for schools?

Perhaps the change can start with talking to employers who would be more interested in workers presenting a portfolio CV that demonstrates skills students have mastered. I should allow employers to read supporting statements from teachers and see the actual work that students have done which demonstrated those skills. Change is happening thanks to pressure from employers but governments are not reacting nearly quickly enough. Traditionally, we've failed to bring business leaders into a conversation but I don't think it's entirely their fault. We've put up physical and metaphorical fences around our schools and we couldn't have done a better job of showing children that this is not real life if we tried.

The School of Communication Arts is a classic example of how the education system doesn't match up to the world of work. Backed lock, stock and barrel by the advertising industry, the programme, which is around the equivalent of a masters, has never been validated by a university, not for lack of trying from the founder, Marc Lewis. Every university has knocked him back saying that he needed a fixed five-year curriculum when the advertising industry doesn't sit still for five minutes never mind five years! Now genuinely part of the advertising industry, the industry defines the curriculum itself and they don't have any teachers or lecturers. People from the industry itself come in and deliver the content themselves. The students are often not even finishing their course before getting snapped up for a job. It shows just how out of step formal education is with how businesses are working in the real world.

Atlas of the Future case study: Generation Democracy

Eighteen x 18

'We vote not only for ourselves, but for "all sons and daughters" and every layer and intersection of identity. We vote for each other.' – Yara Shahidi, Founder

Turning 18 is big news. In the US, you can legally play the lottery, sue someone, buy fireworks – and, of course, vote. Eighteen × 18 exists to make sure coming-of-age voters know what they can vote for, and why it matters.

Actor Yara Shahidi (star of *Black-ish* and *Grown-ish*) was 16 when Donald Trump was elected president of the United States, and she felt the frustration of not being able to vote. She launched Eighteen × 18 in response to that feeling of powerlessness, determined to bring her and her peers' voices to the fore as soon as the law would allow it.

Four million people turned 18 in the US in 2018 (including Yara herself), which meant four million new potential voters. Yara decided to create a platform that would provide down-to-earth, easy-to-understand information on how the government and voting system works, as well as practical details like where to find the nearest polling station, and how to vote from college.

Young voters could use the Eighteen × 18 website to walk through the voter registration process, while explainers and deadline reminders were shared via a newsletter and on social media. The Eighteen × 18 team were also on hand throughout the election to answer questions via direct message or on a dedicated hotline.

They also ran the first #WeVoteNext Summit at the TOMS headquarters in Los Angeles, with an 18-year-old activist from each and every US state. Yara describes it as 'a moment to be in conversation with one another, so that we can figure out what matters to us – because it's what should matter to the US'.

In the end, 2018's US midterms saw a 31 per cent youth turnout – the highest, Yara points out, in 25 years.

In an essay for *Vice*, Yara explains her approach to political engagement: 'If you want to change people's minds about the political issues you care about, you need to have something human for them to understand. If you just explain the theory, or the economic impact, then many won't understand the human element of how policy impacts people.' That's why Eighteen × 18's social media is filled with stories from 18-year-olds from around the country, sharing personal perspectives on why issues like gun violence, disenfranchisement and the opioid epidemic matter.

With Eighteen × 18's first major campaign – around the US midterms – now under its belt, they are looking to the future. With runoffs in many states, plus upcoming governor and senator elections, there's plenty to keep understanding and communicating to an increasingly politically aware youth electorate. Looking ahead following the #WeVoteNext Summit, Yara explains 'it's now about how do we proceed in a way in which our humanity is collectively bettered'.

And this runs deeper than individual elections – it's about more than the next trip to the polling station: 'It's not about waiting to be 18 and voting,' Yara says, 'but being active citizens at every point in your personal evolution. Active citizenship takes so many forms. How can we be involved in policy? How can we be involved in getting to know our representatives? How can we be involved in cultural change? Cultural change is underrated because political change creates such immediate effect, but cultural change has a much more lasting impact. Think about the idea that culture ultimately lasts longer than a generation. That's powerful.'

Discover more online: https://atlasofthefuture.org/project/eighteen-x-18

Project 1: Pupil prime minister

This persuasive writing project leads pupils through writing a political manifesto. It is the perfect way to teach persuasive writing whilst engaging with citizenship and real-world politics.

This project can be made very exciting by splitting the class into two political parties. You may decide to do this by grouping school houses or teams together. Arrange the class into their parties at the start of Lesson 2 and tell pupils they will be working in these parties for the rest of the project.

Lesson 1

Welcome to Pupil Prime Minister! This first lesson helps pupils to get a general overview of politics.

Introduction (10 mins)

Find out what the pupils already know about politics and how the country is run. Run a whole-class discussion, asking pupils to write their ideas directly onto the interactive whiteboard (IWB) file or ask pupils to first talk in pairs and write things they know down on sticky notes.

Main (30 mins)

Split the class into groups. Each group studies up to five aspects of politics in detail from the following list using tablets or laptops if you have them. Alternatively, have pre-prepared resources for them to study. The UK Parliament Education Service website has lots of free resources which are very useful.

- Political parties
- Constituencies

- Voting
- Parliament
- Making laws

Give each group five minutes to make brief notes on the first topic before moving them onto the next bullet point. Make this a quick, time-limited activity using a visible timer to keep them on track and focused.

Plenary (20 mins)

Hold an open, whole-class discussion about what each bullet point means, giving groups time to reach a consensus.

Lesson 2

In this lesson, your class will create two political parties and write a mini-manifesto. N.B. This lesson requires you to split the class into their two political parties.

Introduction (20 mins)

Show an example of a political party manifesto as a video. YouTube has lots of different examples for you to choose from and you can see some created for the Pupil Prime Minister project here: www.youtube.com/playlist?list=PL_odjZ7bN8F7bqieuY9lpmPb1jBB_5xOi.

As a whole class, discuss different sections that need to be thought about when writing a manifesto and summarise the ideas on the IWB under the following headings:

- What values do you represent?
- What problems does the country need to address?
- What are your dreams for the country's future?

Main (20 mins)

Split pupils into groups within their political parties, and tell them to work on what their mini-manifesto will say using the bullet points. Remind them that this is a very general overview and they don't need to go into too much detail. This is a good time to choose a sentence focus for pupils to include in their work.

Plenary (10 mins)

Pupils now, individually, choose the best sentence (or two) for each section of their manifesto:

- What values do you represent?
- What problems does the country need to address?
- What are your dreams for the country's future?

Give pupils five minutes to write out their chosen sentence(s) on a mini-whiteboard, then ask them to practise reading it out loud to a partner.

Filming (10 mins)

Film all three sections from each political party using a tablet or phone. If your pupils have their sentence written on a whiteboard, this can be held next to the camera person so the presenter doesn't need to read from their book. Ideally, filming should be done at the front of the class so that everyone can give feedback on performance.

Lesson 3

In this lesson, your class will explore a political issue and each political party will develop a stance on it.

Teaching tip
Always save your annotated interactive whiteboard files.

Introduction (20 mins)

Choose an issue from the following list:

- transport
- energy
- recycling
- food
- tax
- national service.

As a whole class, discuss the issue and make notes on the board recording what the pupils already know about it. IMPORTANT: Try to keep opinions balanced so that pupils don't form a strong stance on the issue yet before they've had a chance to explore it.

Main (25 mins)

Explain to pupils that they are going to work individually to develop a political stance on the issue using the notes from the whole-class discussion. Pupils can use the following headings to help them draft ideas:

- What we believe in
- What we don't believe in
- Our winning conclusion.

Plenary (15 mins)

Tell pupils to share their work with a partner. Introduce a sentence level focus to the whole class which you will develop in the next lesson. For example, you may wish to demonstrate how to use an IF + THEN sentence for the third bullet point above.

Example

If you want limitless energy, if you would rather see beautiful green fields instead of monstrous wind turbines, then you should vote for the Nuclear Fanatics Party!

In pairs, tell the pupils to rewrite two sentences from their drafts using the sentence level focus. Invite pupils to share their examples with the rest of the class. This is a great time to develop their oratory skills!

Lesson 4

In this lesson, your class will explore a political issue and each political party will develop a stance on it. It is a repeat of Lesson 3 with a different sentence level focus in the plenary. You can repeat this lesson as many times as you like, focusing on a different political issue each time.

Teaching tip

Always save your annotated interactive whiteboard files.

Introduction (20 mins)

Choose an issue from the following list (one you haven't covered previously):

- transport
- energy
- recycling
- food
- tax
- national service.

As a whole class, discuss the issue and make notes on the board recording what the pupils already know about it. IMPORTANT: Try to keep opinions balanced so that pupils don't form a strong stance on the issue yet before they've had a chance to explore it.

Main (25 mins)

Explain to pupils that they are going to work individually to develop a political stance on the issue using the notes from the whole-class discussion. Pupils can use the following headings to help them draft ideas:

- What we believe in
- What we don't believe in
- Our winning conclusion.

Plenary (15 mins)

Tell pupils to share their work with a partner. Introduce another sentence level focus to the whole class which you will develop in the next lesson. For example, you may wish to demonstrate how to use rhetorical questions for the third bullet point above.

Example

Do you want free public transport? Would you like to live in a more peaceful neighbourhood? Do you want cleaner air for our children? Then vote for the EcoBus Drivers Party!

In pairs, tell pupils to rewrite two sentences from their drafts using the sentence level focus. Invite pupils to share their examples with the rest of the class. This is a great time to develop their oratory skills!

Lesson 5

Pupils use their drafts from the previous lessons to write a manifesto with an introduction followed by addressing as many issues as you managed to cover in the previous lessons.

Teaching tip

You could use any recording device for this lesson, including tablets or phones, but ensure you have tested your equipment beforehand. Check how loud or close to the device the pupils need to be for the best results and demonstrate this to the class.

Introduction (10 mins)

As preparation for this lesson, take a photo or scan a pupil's draft from the previous lesson. Use this to do a whole-class edit. Focus on the structure and sentence level work from the previous lessons and up-level their work. In pairs, tell pupils to practise writing an improved section of the chosen piece of work.

Main (25 mins)

Tell pupils to work individually to write the final draft of their manifesto making sure they include sentence level work. Use the three headings as a way to structure their writing into three paragraphs for the introduction and each of the issues that you worked on. Split the number of sections according to ability and time available between the pupils within each political party.

Introduction

- What values do you represent?
- What problems does the country need to address?
- What are your dreams for the country's future?

Issue 1 (e.g. Transport)

- Tell us what you believe in.
- Tell us what you don't believe in.
- Deliver your winning conclusion.

Issue 2 (e.g. Energy)

- Tell us what you believe in.
- Tell us what you don't believe in.
- Deliver your winning conclusion.

Plenary (10 mins)

Choose one pupil from each political party to read each introduction and each issue that they've written about, and record them reading it. You can also record another pupil's introduction from each party for the closing of the manifesto as they are essentially just a reaffirmation of party values.

Teaching tip

The videos could either be filmed straight to camera or you could record them as voice-overs used alongside images that relate to each section.

Chapter 2
Kitchen kid

Introduction

The World Health Organization (WHO) has identified obesity as one of the most serious global public health challenges of the 21st century (WHO, 2018). Though recent reports (Abarca-Gómez et al., 2017) indicate that rising trends in child body mass index (BMI) since 1975 have recently begun to plateau, levels of obesity in the UK are alarmingly high. In fact, they are the highest in the whole of Western Europe (OECD, 2017).

The figures speak for themselves: according to the Royal College of Paediatrics and Child Health, almost one in every five children are overweight or obese when they start primary school, while as many as one in three are overweight by the time they start secondary school.

In this chapter...

In this chapter we will explore the effects that obesity can have on children and how it is our responsibility to help educate about the importance of having a healthy diet. We hear from the renowned British food writer and author Bee Wilson and inspiring headteacher of Washingborough Academy Jason O'Rourke who is studying for a Diploma in Education focusing on food education. They share their innovative and passionate perspectives on how they are changing the food landscape for young people through their platforms such as TastEd and the food education curriculum. Additionally, we learn in the Atlas of the Future case study how tech startup, NotPla, has approached the single-use plastic crisis by creating a completely compostable, biodegradable or edible water bottle made of seaweed. There are many good discussion points to take from these aspects before embarking on the six-lesson Kitchen Kid project where the children will learn more about cooking and nutrition, culminating in recording their very own cooking competition!

How does being overweight affect children?

Being an overweight or obese child undeniably results in significant immediate problems. At a developmental level, obesity can cause poor bone health and breathing disorders in a child (RCPCH, undated). Obese children are also less likely to be active. A reduction in their opportunities to enjoy physical activity may have subsequent impacts on their physical, mental and emotional wellbeing.

Children may experience further loss of self-esteem and self-confidence if they encounter negative attitudes to obesity from their peers and in wider society. This manifests itself in many ways, often very publicly. For example, a UK newspaper recently reported on the modern rise of 'obesophobia', in which people shame and blame obese people for their condition, through social media channels (Monbiot, 2018).

Of course, there are also long-term impacts of childhood obesity, too. Obese children who go on to become obese adults will face increased risk of health conditions such as heart disease, stroke, high blood pressure, diabetes and some cancers (RCPCH, undated).

The UK government has taken steps to address the issue of child obesity, announcing in their obesity action plan in 2016 that they would encourage primary school children to eat more healthily and stay active.

Talking point

What do you think a healthy diet looks like? What do you like to do to stay active? How could the school promote a healthier lifestyle?

Perhaps surprisingly though, research suggests that unhealthy weight gain in children may not actually be determined by their activity levels (Wilks et al., 2011). It seems that while being active is important for overall health, it does not necessarily make you less likely to become obese. In fact, it appears that obesity is simply a cause of inactivity, rather than a consequence of it.

So, if inactivity isn't a major cause of obesity in children, what is causing them to gain unhealthy weight? Research has been carried out into a variety of reasons that range from genetic factors, from the use of antibiotics, through to exposure to endocrine-disrupting chemicals present in many pesticides and household products.

One thing that scientists are sure of is that, of all the factors identified to date, diet remains the most important known driver of weight gain. Specifically, cheap, energy-dense and nutrient-poor foods and drinks are thought by many to be at fault. This is reflected in the UK government's obesity strategy, the first strand of which aims to encourage industry to cut sugar in food and drinks.

In schools, we are in the privileged position of being positive influencers for the children in our classes. There is no better place to encourage the benefits of living a healthy life, and what this looks like for them now and in the future, than in school. It is our responsibility to educate the children on what healthy looks like. We should be aiming to increase the children's health knowledge so they can create positive attitudes towards their own wellbeing. Providing children with a health education is more likely to help them lead a long and healthy life. Additionally, we know that having a well-nourished body leads to a well-nourished mind which is optimal for learning.

Improving food literacy should sit neatly alongside traditional literacy, helping children deepen their understanding of food, science and culture. It also offers meaningful life skills as they learn to prepare balanced meals and snacks. Teaching children how to listen to hunger and fullness cues and how to provide the body with the right amounts of the right foods is imperative for their future health longevity.

We should be introducing them to new foods from around the world, expanding their knowledge about where foods come from, what they look and feel like and what they taste like. They need to understand that all foods have a place in their diet and that what they put in their mouths has some kind of effect on their body. We also need to educate them on the persuasive way food agencies and the media promote foods and drinks and to be curious and question the authenticity of what they see and hear.

Diet is just one aspect of a healthy life, but a great starting point. It is an aspect that they can get their teeth into – literally!

Interview with Bee Wilson and Jason O'Rourke

Introducing...

Bee Wilson is a food writer and historian. Her books include *Consider the Fork: A History of How We Cook and Eat* and, most recently, *First Bite: How We Learn to Eat* (Fourth Estate), about the psychology of eating and how we can change our diets for the better.

Jason O'Rourke is the headteacher of Washingborough Academy and an EdD student researching food education and school leadership. He is the Trustee of TastEd and was the Caroline Walker Trust's 'Food Hero of the Year' in 2019.

Why are you passionate about food education?

Bee: Eating is not something we are born knowing how to do, like breathing. Our preferences for certain foods are something we learn and sometimes have to unlearn. The sad thing in today's world is that the main educator of a child's palate is the food industry, which has encouraged a generation of children to gravitate towards foods that are sweet, fatty, salty and ultra-processed. We need to redress the balance and make a child see the joys in other flavours and textures, from the bitterness of grapefruit to the hard crunch of a carrot.

When I was researching my book *First Bite: How We Learn to Eat*, I came across a study from Turkey that stopped me in my tracks. It suggested that the single greatest predictor of the way a person eats aged 20 – from whether they are picky to whether they enjoy vegetables – is the way that he or she ate at the age of two. This really brought home to me that so many of our attitudes to food are set at a very early age. School is a very rare and powerful opportunity in a person's life when whatever preferences they have learned at home can be circumvented and it is possible for a person to discover tastes they never knew they had.

Jason: The key to any person learning is to tap into areas of interest, and with children, things that they are familiar with. We started to develop our food education curriculum a number of years ago. You want children to learn through experience and food is one of those very rare areas that everyone has experience with – good and bad. We all hopefully eat three times a day at least, so to be creative in this area and encourage other areas of learning around food is a great way to engage children. Also, as a headteacher, I am passionate about the joy of food and wanted to bring that feeling to the children within the school.

What has changed, if at all, to make food such an important topic these days?

Bee: Food has always been an important topic; it's just that general opinion is finally starting to catch up. When I started out as a food writer 20 years ago, I endlessly had people telling me that what I was doing was trivial. I remember working a reception class in Cambridge and we were talking about loud and quiet foods – crunchy and soft. One boy said to me, 'I can't eat crunchy foods.' I was surprised and asked why. He opened his mouth and his teeth were blackened stumps. I felt so sorry that at the age of five his food choices were already limited by the fact that he had consumed a sugary diet. Poor diets are causing huge amounts of completely preventable human suffering, and it's not right. I don't get those trivial comments so much anymore. I think we are all starting to recognise that food is political, and that the food we eat has huge ramifications both for our own health and for the world we live in.

Jason: I think that food has developed a much higher profile in the UK with a focus on seasonal produce, artisan local foods and its exposure in the media; however, this has not been seen across the educational landscape. The inclusion of food-related learning within the UK national curriculum is very limited indeed and we have a lack of skills base within the teaching profession because of this. Basic cooking skills have not been part of the primary curriculum at all, so the generations that have passed through our school system are not confident in their own skills and as it is not explicitly taught at primary schools, it is not seen as important as traditional subjects such as English and maths. I have often said that a child's knowledge of fronted adverbials is not going to lengthen their life span, but knowledge about how food can have a positive effect on your health and wellbeing can.

How do we get real, sustainable food to be as desirable as junk food?

Bee: This is a question I think about a lot. It's perfectly possible for a person to grow up and desire a bowl of deep orange pumpkin soup or a platter of delicious Asian greens wok fried with soy sauce and garlic, but the problem is that our culture still speaks of vegetables as a kind of punishment and we have a whole system of celebration in the UK centred around sugar (think of the television programme *The Great British Bake Off*).

We tend to focus far too much on the mouth and what a child puts in his or her mouth. By allowing them to explore food with the other senses, it takes the pressure off and a child is able to use his or her natural curiosity to get to know a food a bit. I've had comments such as, 'I've never felt an onion before.' I found that mind blowing. It wasn't just that they hadn't tasted an onion, but they had never actually felt that papery skin. How can you know if you will like an onion if you have never felt one? It's amazing to see a classroom of children taking their first bite of lemon or celery. And often, the power of positive peer pressure means that often they do like it, even on first bite. But not liking is also fine. The huge thing is to feel brave enough to try.

Jason: Giving children exposure to healthier foods is the key. If a parent does not like broccoli or spinach, they will not expose their child to it at home, so the child will not know if they like it. Through the lessons that we do in school, we encourage children to explore new foods through their senses, with no expectation to actual taste/eat the food. However, we find that the children do want to taste as they are naturally curious and, having 'explored' the food with their other senses, they want to know what it tastes like. Through this method, children are learning the joy of food and are trying things such as anchovies, olives, herring, chillies, and so on.

Atlas of the Future case study: Edible water bottles

Ooho!

The consumption of non-renewable resources for single-use items and the amount of waste generated is profoundly unsustainable. That's why London-based tech startup NotPla wants to make packaging disappear. They have created a water 'bottle' you can eat.

Ooho! is a natural packaging made of seaweed, entirely compostable and biodegradable. Inspired by egg yolks, water is trapped inside layers made up of brown algae and calcium chloride and can be drunk when those membranes are punctured. The membranes have been compared to the skin of an apple, as they can then be eaten or thrown away.

The goal is to create a waste-free alternative to plastic bottles, cups and sachets with a material that is as cheap as plastic and can encapsulate most liquids including water, soft drinks, spirits and condiments.

In April 2019, London Marathon trialled Oohos for the first time on a major scale, sponsored by Lucozade. The pods provided runners with a few gulps of Lucozade for a thirst-quenching pop. Water-filled Oohos are popping up at races all over the UK, and the company expect a major trial of the first seaweed-based ketchup sachets to happen in the next six months!

'Fixing the future means ensuring that cities are sustainable by having good infrastructure (transport and waste) to enable people to commute, shop and live sustainably without impacting the environment.' – Lise Honsinger, CFO, NotPla

Discover more online: https://atlasofthefuture.org/project/ooho

Project 2: Kitchen kid

Over the next five lessons, you'll be teaching pupils about cooking and nutrition before getting them to film their own recipe for their very own cooking competition show, 'Kitchen Kid'!

Lesson 1

This lesson introduces the project with a bang! You're going to prepare some food in the classroom and film it. Before the lesson, you will need to decide on a recipe and have the ingredients ready. I recommend finding a 'no cook' recipe to keep things nice and simple. For example, salads, sandwiches and wraps are all easy to make. Here are some examples:

- https://greatist.com/eat/mason-jar-recipes
- www.bbcgoodfood.com/recipes/stripy-houmous-salad-jars

- www.bbcgoodfood.com/recipes/693641/avocado-salad
- www.bbcgoodfood.com/recipes/4714/mexican-bean-salad
- www.bbcgoodfood.com/recipes/kale-bulghar-tabbouleh-yogurt-dressing
- www.bbcgoodfood.com/recipes/11199/quinoa-lentil-and-feta-salad

Teaching tip

To see what your final video will look like, watch this example video: www.youtube.com/watch?v=_BCFRsfa6rU

Introduction (10 mins)

Ask pupils if they have seen any cookery shows on television. If so, which ones? Hold a whole-class discussion about them, especially those with a competitive element between teams or individuals (for example, *The Great British Bake Off*). Talk about how they work, what the format is and why they are so popular.

Main (40 mins)

The main body of the lesson can be run in different ways, depending on the resources, groups and number of adults you have. The important part is to ensure that, by the end of the lesson, there are video clips of each section of the recipe being made.

Do one of the following:

- Make one example of the recipe at the front of the class, inviting children to the front to carry out the different steps. Read the instructions aloud and film each step.
- Split the class into groups of roughly three to five. Each group makes the recipe, carrying out all the steps themselves as the teacher reads out the instructions and each group does their own filming.
- Split the class into groups of three to five. Each group makes the recipe, carrying out all the steps themselves, but you film different sections with different groups to make one whole-class film.

Using Adobe Spark Video, it is very easy to add voice-overs to the video clips, so allow the pupils to concentrate on cooking rather than explaining what they are doing to camera at the same time.

Now that you have each step of your recipe on video, load these clips into an Adobe Spark Video project. This will be really useful to have in time for the final lesson when you record your voice-overs for each step of your Kitchen Kid video.

Plenary (10 mins)

Make notes on a flip chart, working wall or any other way of recording ideas that you use which pupils can refer to in subsequent lessons. Recap the key steps of the recipe in order. For each key step, collect ideas of imperative verbs and adverbs of manner which could be used in later lessons when writing up the recipe. For example:

- Carefully mix…
- Finely chop...
- Stir quickly…
- Generously spread...

Lesson 2

This lesson looks at the features of instruction writing (recipes), using both video and printed texts. Before the lesson, prepare a set of printed instructions for a simple recipe, for example, scrambled eggs. Cut up the recipe, dividing it into the different stages. You'll also need to prepare printouts of the recipes from the two videos listed in the main part of the lesson. The links to the recipe instructions are in the YouTube video descriptions.

Introduction (10 mins)

Place the cut-up instructions in a bag or hat. Choose a pupil to draw out an instruction from the bag or hat, one at a time, and read it out. Tell the rest of the class to write the instructions on a mini-whiteboard or piece of paper as they are pulled out. Once all of the instructions have been pulled out, tell the class to follow the recipe. This will be difficult because they will be out of order. Now ask the children to put them in order. Discuss whether the instructions were clear, easy to follow and put in the correct order. If not, why not?

Main (30 mins)

Show the class these video recipe clips from BBC Good Food:

> How to make pancakes:
> www.youtube.com/watch?v=QyWTHVvlBTw
> How to make the perfect scrambled eggs:
> www.youtube.com/watch?v=smYfx1r6eYI

As a whole class, study the instructions in the videos above. What makes them easy to follow? What type of language is used? Make notes on the board.

Now give out a printed recipe to each table or group and tell them to compare it to the video recipe they've just watched. Challenge children to find the following in the printed recipes:

Option 1 (easier)

- Imperative verbs: 'bossy' verbs which give an order or command, for example, chop, put, mix or heat.
- Adverbs of manner: these give more information about how to do the verb, for example, carefully or quickly.
- A summary sentence: lets the reader know they have completed the recipe, for example, 'When the cake is golden brown and shrinking away from the edges of the tin, then you will have a delicious treat ready for teatime!'

Option 2 (more challenging)
As above, plus:

- Two-step instructions: where the sentence contains two linked actions, for example, 'Add in the flour and stir quickly until the ingredients are thoroughly mixed.'
- Consequence instructions: where one action depends on the outcome of another, for example, 'Once the eggs have begun to set, loosen them from the bottom of the pan with a spatula.'

Plenary (20 mins)

This is a chance for your pupils to write draft cooking instructions for your class recipe. Choose something simple like a sandwich or a no-cook salad. This can also be done as a group activity or a whole-class modelled write. Practise using some of the sentence level work above.

Lesson 3

Pupils write instructions for the recipe you made in Lesson 1. Have a picture of a pupil's recipe from Lesson 2 ready for whole-class editing.

Introduction (15 mins)

Display a pupil's written recipe from Lesson 2 for whole-class editing. Discuss whether the instructions are clear and easy to follow. If not, why? Revisit the sentence level work from Lesson 2 to see if there are any examples in this recipe.

Option 1 (easier)

- Imperative verbs: 'bossy' verbs which give an order or command, for example, chop, put, mix or heat.

- Adverbs of manner: these give more information about how to do the verb, for example, carefully or quickly.
- A summary sentence: lets the reader know they have completed the recipe, for example, 'When the cake is golden brown and shrinking away from the edges of the tin, then you will have a delicious treat ready for teatime!'

Option 2 (more challenging)
As above, plus:

- Two-step instructions: where the sentence contains two linked actions, for example, 'Add in the flour and stir quickly until the ingredients are thoroughly mixed.'
- Consequence instructions: where one action depends on the outcome of another, for example, 'Once the eggs have begun to set, loosen them from the bottom of the pan with a spatula.'

Main (35 mins)

Sentence level work (10 mins): As a whole class, recap the recipe you made in Lesson 1 and break it down into four sections on the board. Generate a word bank on the IWB of useful verbs, adverbs, adjectives and so on for each section in note form.

Writing task (25 mins): Ask pupils to work individually to write up their instructions using the sentence level work.

Plenary (10 mins)

Peer-editing and improving with a partner. Each child looks for success in their partner's writing and, if appropriate, makes suggestions for improvement. Partners could also use a thesaurus to up-level vocabulary choices, taking care to use precise language rather than overly 'flowery' language.

Share a successful recipe step from each group. Can others explain why they are so good? Can others suggest ways to improve their sentences?

Lesson 4

In this lesson, pupils work collaboratively to produce a three-part introduction to their Kitchen Kid cookery show.

Introduction (5 mins)

Show the class the example video which introduces the programme:
www.youtube.com/watch?v=_BCFRsfa6rU

Discuss the key elements of the delivery:

- a bubbly presenter to start off the programme and keep viewers watching
- an enthusiastic introduction to the two teams or chefs
- a tantalising description of what is to come in the show... the delicious food!

Main (50 mins)

Sentence level work (15 mins): Making notes on the board, discuss how to use adjectives and adverbs for an introduction with impact. Get pupils to work in pairs and come up with verbal examples for the three sections you discussed in the first part of the lesson and make notes on the board of the most useful examples.

Upper Key Stage 2
As an extension, a 'with/who...' clause can be added.

Example

'Spicy, aromatic pizza **with** mozzarella oozing slowly from the thick, crispy crust.'

'I'm a passionate cook **who** prefers to bake mouth-watering pies rather than tell intricate lies.'

Make notes on the IWB and develop pairs' ideas as a whole class so that pupils can have some ideas to work with in the following writing task.

Writing (20 mins): Now tell pupils to work on a couple of sentences for each section of the introduction:

- a welcome to the programme
- an introduction to the contestants or teams
- a description of the food from Lesson 1
- an end to the introduction using rhetorical questions.

Edit and improve (15 mins): Peer-editing and improving with a partner. Each child looks for success in their partner's writing and, if appropriate, makes suggestions for improvement. Partners could also use a thesaurus to up-level vocabulary choices, taking care to use precise language rather than overly flowery language.

Plenary (5 mins)

Share a success from each group. Can others explain why their introduction is so good? Can others suggest ways to improve their sentences?

Lesson 5

In this lesson, pupils will write an 'outro' for their Kitchen Kid cooking show before recording voice-overs for a whole-class video.

Introduction (10 mins)

Discuss what needs to be included at the end of your show so that your pupils have a good idea of the style of their writing task before attempting it themselves.

Teaching tip

You can watch the example video again if necessary, although remind pupils that they shouldn't copy it, but improve it!

Tell pupils they should include:

- a summary of the meal
- congratulations to the chefs on their fantastic food
- a closing statement and goodbye.

Give pairs some time to rehearse ideas verbally for how they will end the show and invite them to share their ideas with the whole class.

Main (35 mins)

Whole-class work (15 mins): Remind children of the recipe they made in Lesson 1. Use mini-whiteboards so that partners or small groups can work together to write down at least two expanded noun phrases to describe the food, for example, 'colourful and mouth-watering wrap'.

On the board, make a list of expanded noun phrases in a sentence to describe the food so that the whole class has a range of phrases to choose from in the writing task. Do the same for the next two sections of the outro so that there is a clear framework in which pupils can structure their writing.

Example

'The chefs really have pulled out all the stops in making this healthy and nutritious wrap!'

A possible extension task is to challenge the children to include a parenthesis in their work and/or expanded noun phrases.

Example

'This colourful and mouth-watering wrap – made in less than 10 minutes – is a perfect lunchtime snack.'

'The chefs (who worked beautifully as a team) really made our mouths water with their healthy and nutritious wrap!'

Writing (20 mins): Tell pupils to write their outros using the IWB as a source of ideas. Remind them to include a summary of the meal, congratulations to the chefs and a closing statement and goodbye.

Plenary (15 mins)

The Kitchen Kid show format will be:

- programme introduction
- recipe step 1
- recipe step 2
- recipe step 3
- recipe step 4
- programme outro.

Invite pupils to read one section of their writing aloud from the project and record them as voice-overs in Adobe Spark Video on top of the video clips that you filmed in the first lesson. Watch your video back as a class and take feedback on performances and the video as a whole.

Now that you have finished a Spark Video, share it with your pupils so they duplicate it before editing their own version with all their own voice-overs, choice of titles, captions and so on, in an ICT lesson.

Lesson 6

In this lesson, pupils will select writing for rehearsing and then film their very own Kitchen Kid cooking show.

Introduction (10 mins)

Remind the class of the intended outcome of this project: to make a TV programme, Kitchen Kid, which shows how to cook a recipe but also includes information about eating healthily. The format of the show is:

- programme introduction
- recipe step 1
- recipe step 2
- recipe step 3
- recipe step 4
- programme outro.

Teaching tip

This lesson can be organised in different ways depending on how many finished films you want to make. The instructions are for making one class film but it is easy enough to get each group to produce one film each.

As a class, give out the different sections to different groups to take charge of. Don't forget, you already filmed the cooking steps in Lesson 1 so you are using the writing to record voice-overs for each of those steps. Assign roles for different pupils for each section. Having two children or more share lines is absolutely fine and it actually keeps it interesting.

Roles required:

- tablet operator
- director
- actor(s).

Main (40 mins)

Rehearsal (10 mins): Allow groups time to rehearse their work. Discuss how to read aloud with good expression and volume, also noting that TV voices are usually a little larger than life!

Filming (30 mins): Invite groups, section by section, to the front of the class in order to film or record voice-overs of their work. Invite the whole class to give feedback on performances after each section.

Plenary (10 mins)

If you have time and are recording directly into something like Adobe Spark, share the draft video with the class taking feedback on performance and things to improve on before the final export.

Chapter 3
Conscious consumers

Introduction

Move over, millennials. After being depicted as 'entitled' and accused of 'ruining' several industries, the generation that newspapers love to hate is officially no longer the centre of attention. Instead, it is now Generation Z's turn to inform the trends and shape the market.

Gone are the days of having an opinion and simply sharing it amongst friends, or to a few in writing. In this world of accessible technology and social media, your voice can literally be heard by many, at the press of a button. Now it is possible to have an opinion, make it known and build a following, shaming those who don't conform along the way too. Nowadays, you cannot help but see evidence of these worthy campaigns wherever you go, such as that against single-use plastic. Generation Z are here to make a difference and shout about it.

In this chapter...

In this chapter we will unpack who Generation Z are and how they are influencing consumerism in a socially conscious way. Hil Berg, Iceland Foods' lead on sustainability and corporate social responsibility strategy, shares her insights for growing a culture of responsibility, sustainability and corporate activism and we learn from shoe brand Veja's continuing journey in the world of sustainable fashion. Having been inspired by these forward-thinking and passionate advocates of putting purpose before profit, empower your children to do the same through the five-lesson Conscious Consumers project.

So who, exactly, are Generation Z?

Generation Z (or Gen Z), defined as anyone born after 1996 or 1997, is the youngest generation in the UK, having a huge impact on cultural, commercial and social trends. In 2020, Gen Z accounts for 40 per cent of all consumers. That's a lot of pressure for a generation whose members are currently 24 years old or younger, but Gen Zs seem to be taking it in their stride.

Share with the class

Also called post-millennials and iGeneration, Gen Z are used to being 'on' all the time. In contrast to millennials, they never experienced a life without an internet connection and smartphone technology. A smartphone-first generation, Gen Zs are nevertheless using five screens per person (the other four being the TV, desktop computer, laptop and tablet). As a result, it has been calculated that by the time they are 15 years old, they will have already been exposed to some 200,000 marketing messages.

Not only is the newest UK generation extremely tech-savvy, they've also become immune to most advertising methods and have a low tolerance for adverts in general. Out of the 12 million people currently blocking ads in the UK, the largest chunk are members of the Gen Z generation. The majority of Gen Zs also prefer streaming content to watching television, specifically via services such as Netflix and Spotify, where there are either no adverts by design, or the influx of adverts can be controlled by upgrading to a premium membership.

Gen Zs predominantly use social media for content consumption and entertainment or, as the term is becoming known, 'infotainment' (material that is intended to inform and entertain). It is their preferred place to not only interact with brands and experience content, but also to produce content of their own (one in four Gen Zs have their own YouTube channel). Also, Gen Zs are as likely to 'follow' an influencer on social media as they are to 'follow' their friends.

Talking point

What is social media? Do members of your family use social media? What do they mostly use it for?

It's not only the hyper-digital habits of Gen Z that are disrupting the market, however. First and foremost, it is their values — and how vocal they are about them.

How the Gen Z mindset is affecting corporate social responsibility

Gen Z are the ultimate conscious consumers. Precisely because they are being exposed to advertising and marketing messages all their lives, they have developed a clear preference for brands with a personality; brands that are perceived as authentic and honest; brands whose values align with theirs. Where millennials tend to favour brand recognition, with Gen Z what matters is the message.

This has resulted in an interesting shift in brand positioning. A company communicating a lifestyle of unattainable perfection will be much less successful with Gen Zs than a company that comes off as raw and real. And as Gen Z, like millennials, appear to be less prone to consumerism than previous generations, they make decisions on where they will spend their money, not based on a brand name, but rather on what that brand represents.

Being ethical in their practice, sustainable in their production and manufacturing, environmentally friendly and vocal about social issues, is what sets a brand apart in Gen Z's eyes. So much so that more than nine out of ten millennials and Gen Zs would forsake or even boycott a brand in favour of another, if that other was associated with a 'good' cause.

More specifically, Gen Zs are looking for brands that contribute to a better planet and the betterment of society, by solving existing problems; brands with a mission to make a difference, who are vocal about their endeavours; brands that help their customers become part of their mission, by giving back and being involved in activities that promote social causes. The UK's youngest generation is making sure that corporate social responsibility (CSR) is more than just an obscure reference on a company's website: it's a company's *raison d'être*.

Talking point

Which brands stand out as supporting good causes? What is different about their messaging?

This turn to conscious consumerism affects not only the brand's advertising approach, but also their actual products and offerings. As Gen Z is so forthcoming with their opinions about a brand (often using aggressive practices such as 'calling out' perceived malpractices on social media), companies find themselves facing an interesting conundrum: to keep making a profit, they need to start behaving more like non-profit companies.

What businesses are doing to appeal to conscious consumers

There are a multitude of ways to be a profitable company while at the same time contributing to making life on our planet better. These range from using a portion of profits to sponsor a worthy cause or charity, creating great working conditions for personnel and sourcing materials ethically or locally or switching to practices that are less harmful for the environment. All these aspects make a brand 'meaningful' – and Havas Group research showed that, in the last decade, 'meaningful' brands have outperformed other brands in the stock market by 206 per cent.

Share with the class

A gleaming example of such a change is Adidas, who pledged to switch completely to recycled plastic by 2024 and created the 'UltraBoost' shoe line, made from ocean plastic – and subsequently sold out of all one million pairs. Unilever is also pushing its sustainable brands, which see a 50 per cent faster growth than its other products. IKEA is doing the same, and making about £1.47 billion in sustainable product sales. Thanks to Gen Z, being an ethically good business is good for business.

Interview with Hil Berg

Introducing...

Hil Berg leads on sustainability and CSR strategy at Iceland Foods, advising the board and working on partnerships and communications. She was previously Head of Public Relations for the company in the 1990s and early 2000s, directing communications for the 'Food You Can Trust' campaign, which encompassed a ban on GM Food, the removal of artificial additives and other industry-leading initiatives.

What is it about consumer culture that Iceland is looking to change?

There's a growing culture of responsibility which is reflected in the journey of Iceland. We're now in a place where there are a whole host of wicked problems assailing us. For us, that means we have to meet the challenge head on, collaborate and start making things happen by taking ownership of our operations. For the last few years, we've seen a significant dip in trust in institutions as shown by the Edelman Trust barometer. But this year in the UK, there's been a 19 per cent increase in trust in businesses, which is huge. We think that we've got a really significant role to play in looking at how we can be profitable in a highly responsible way and making a hugely positive contribution to society. Our palm oil drive was an example of that but our staff are also pushing us to make a difference around poverty, single-use plastics and taking an active role in our local community. Our employees are our local community because over 80 per cent live within three miles of our shops. We look to our staff to help us set our agenda and find solutions. Our people are our engine room which fuels our responsible plan and our corporate activism.

At the height of our palm oil campaigning in 2018, two young sisters got involved and decided to target Kelloggs for their use of palm oil. They started a petition against Kelloggs and ended up in the boardroom talking with the senior executives. That's an amazing example of how the public, two young girls, can have a huge impact without having any purchasing power themselves.

Why is Iceland leading the charge on ethical and sustainable business?

The stuff we're doing around sustainability is genuinely not about achieving sales. It's not part of a cynical sales drive or greenwashing or part of a commercial thing. It's driven by our CEO and our staff who want to do the right thing and take a firm moral stance. But it also has a huge impact on the kinds of people who want to work for us, our recruitment and retention process, not to mention that they are our sales people and if they feel good about working for us, that's going to have a long-term positive impact on profits. It's having a huge impact because we're attracting millennials who choose to work for us because it satisfies their desire to work for a company with meaning and be part of something which makes a difference.

In terms of collaboration, our approach is designed to try and inspire other business to take a similar approach with an issue which is close to their hearts, perhaps one that is particular to their manufacturing methods or buying practices so that, as a collective effort, we can be tackling a number of issues all at the same time.

Why is it so important to communicate what you're doing to your audience of current and future shoppers?

The best companies put purpose before profit to make huge positive changes in the world. Your customers decide whether you live or die and you've got a responsibility to serve them in the right way.

We should be encouraging children to ask questions all the time about what they're doing and why they're doing it, to question the brands that they like and the things they buy. We can only really make this world a better place by decreasing rampant consumerism and by getting people to vote with their wallets and stick with the businesses that are more responsible. We're lucky at Iceland in a way, because we're in food and it's something that we'll always need but, at the same time, food waste is absolutely off the charts. We're obsessed as a company with how much food we waste and we want to be part of the change not only in our shops but in the homes of our customers where the majority of food waste happens.

Children can have such a hugely influential effect on adult shopping habits. No one can refuse a child and so, if we can educate them, then what kind of change could we bring about? Think about Easter time when children are given Easter eggs which are a criminal source of plastic waste! If children asked for eggs without the plastic, imagine what an impact that would have at Easter! IKEA has invented a flat-pack egg that you build yourself, which is genius! If kids refused eggs wrapped in plastic, the industry would be forced to change for good and only a six-year-old can wield that kind of power!

I really believe that this generation has the potential to be the special generation and turn things around because they not only have the awareness but they have the passion and they also have the ideas to back it up. If we're going to make the kind of changes we need, then we need to encourage these children as much as possible to feel empowered enough to take action. The rise of Greta Thunberg is so positive and, coupled with things like Extinction Rebellion, this is a level of activism I've not seen since the Nike riots in the eighties. Are we entering a different place where people will actually vote with their wallets? I certainly hope so because the adult generation has silently but knowingly watched the destruction of the planet for decades!

Consumers have much more potential to disrupt than they realise. But so do teachers. They are the unsung heroes of society and heroes to so many children influencers and potential activists. They can be the ones who shape a generation of children, which over time changes society by fostering enquiring minds and developing children who ask questions and think about their decisions.

Atlas of the Future case study: The vegan show in Vogue

Veja shoes

'These sneakers were designed with silk sourced from the Brazilian producer Hermès uses.'

So ran the Vogue headline in an article that put Emma Watson, Eddie Redmayne and Paris-based sustainable sneaker brand Veja in the same sentence. You can consider these green kicks Hollywood-approved footwear. That's because Veja is changing the sustainable fashion game with sneakers that not only look good at an affordable price, but don't unnecessarily damage the environment. They even have a vegan range.

The raw silk yarn in their conscious kicks comes from Bratac, who supplies Hermès. With cotton also sourced from north-eastern Brazil, Veja works with 320 small-scale farmers and their families who use organic farming methods – that means no agro-chemicals or pesticides. Known as 'agroecology', the farmers use methods such as rotation farming and contour planting to preserve the fragile soils.

The farmers work together, pooling their harvests in the same warehouse to minimise the costs. Veja pays them a premium price for their cotton, as well as an end-of-harvest premium which goes towards improving their standard of living. In a similar style to their cotton, Veja works with 60 'Seringeiros' or rubber farmers in the Amazon rainforest, the only place on earth where rubber trees grow in the wild. Using a new technology which allows them to transform the latex into rubber sheets locally, the Seringeiros are able to sell the semi-finished products for a higher income.

This income is also above market price, which Veja hopes will act as an incentive for farmers to pursue rubber farming, because historically many have turned to more destructive pursuits such as cattle-raising and wood extraction due to the low price of petroleum-based synthetic rubber undercutting prices. But their conscientious ethics don't stop there. They don't advertise anywhere, subsequently using the revenue saved to pay their farmers and producers fairly, and because their fabrication costs are three to four times higher than other footwear brands, this still allows them to sell their shoes at a competitive price.

Veja also tightly controls production, only producing orders made six months in advance meaning no extra stock is produced. They strive to reduce CO_2 emissions, transporting their shoes from Porto Alegre in Brazil to Le Havre in France by boat and then by barges along canals to the Parisian suburbs.

'Veja is an investigation, a project that is constantly evolving.' Now, even though we've spent the last paragraphs singing its praises, Veja is by no means perfect. In fact, the brand itself has a whole page outlining why. But it's this level of awareness and determination to improve which makes them a flagship for the future-focused businesses of the world.

Discover more online: https://atlasofthefuture.org/project/veja-shoes

Project 3: #TeamTap

Welcome to the first lesson of this five-lesson non-chronological report-writing sequence. The aim is to use the report-writing to create an informative video about single-use plastic bottles and tap water.

Lesson 1

In this lesson, pupils will engage with the topic via group discussion before researching facts for their own reports.

Before the lesson, you may wish to prepare a selection of books, newspaper clippings or infographics from the internet about water consumption and plastic bottles. Five quality resources would be ideal.

Introduction (15 mins)

Discuss how pupils currently consume water. Introduce the questions below one by one and allow pupils time to discuss their answers in pairs or groups before coming together as a whole class to feed back. You may want them to write notes as they chat and then write up the most useful ones on the board for later use.

- How many of you use disposable water bottles?
- How many of you recycle or reuse your bottles?
- What's the difference between bottled water and tap water?
- Do you know what happens to plastic bottles if you throw them away?
- How are plastic bottles produced?

Main (25 mins)

Ask the class to research facts for the non-chronological report-writing, focusing on single-use plastic bottles, tap water and plastic pollution. If you have pre-prepared resources, challenge your pupils to make a note of the most interesting piece of information in each resource.

Stop the class for mini-plenaries to share facts as a whole class.

Plenary (20 mins)

Ask each group or set of partners to share some of the insights they got from their research. Every time a piece of research is shared, generate some discussion and develop their understanding further. Make notes on the board of the most insightful discussions, questions and statements from the class. These will be useful in the next few lessons so make sure you save your notes.

Spend some time deciding as a class who the audience for your written work and video will be. Who can bring about change in the use of single-use plastic bottles? Children? Parents? The government? Businesses?

Lesson 2

In this lesson, pupils look at the key features of a non-chronological report, a modelled or shared paragraph is written collaboratively and pupils write a paragraph of their own.

Before the lesson, print and copy the example text 'Bottled water: The truth' on pages 38–9 (also available to download from the online resources). Make sure you have one per pair or small group. You need to decide in advance the word, sentence level or grammar focus for this lesson, based on the list of what is included in the example text.

Introduction (10 mins)

Use the example text as a mini guided-reading exercise: you could ask pupils to read sections independently, read with a partner or read aloud, and you could model reading some sections. Discuss any vocabulary the pupils are unfamiliar with and talk in general terms about the layout of the text.

Main (40 mins)

Find examples in the text (10 mins): Using the example text, look more closely at the word, sentence or grammar focus that you've chosen for the lesson from the list below. Challenge pupils to find as many of them as possible in the text. For example, how many generalisers, imperatives and expanded noun phrases can you find?

Feature	Simple	Higher level
Generalisers	most, some	the majority, consumers, the general public
Connectives and conjunctions	coordination – and, so subordination – because	furthermore, in addition
Rhetorical question	Do you like the idea of drinking plastic particles?	Surely it is our consumer right to know how they are checking the water?
Verbs	imperatives: join, help	modals: should, could, may
Emotive or powerful vocabulary	terrible, awful	catastrophic, devastating
Punctuation	possessive apostrophe, commas to separate items in a list	colon to introduce a list
Tense	present – 'people are'	present perfect – 'there have been'
Description	expanded noun phrases – 'their own kitchen'	expanded noun phrases – 'fresh spring water sources'

Modelled writing (10 mins): Model a short, non-chronological report paragraph about one fact from Lesson 1. Include the chosen word, sentence or grammar focus.

Writing (20 mins): Using the word, sentence or grammar focus, pupils write two paragraphs about two different facts from Lesson 1. This works well if you assign two facts to each table. You may want to give different groups different facts so that you have a range of different content for putting together your video by the end of the project.

Plenary (10 mins)

Refocus the pupils on the chosen word, sentence or grammar focus by sharing pupil examples on the board. Ask pupils to show a talk partner where they have successfully used the focus in their own writing, before sharing more examples with the whole class.

Bottled water: The truth

Introduction

Drinking water, sold in plastic bottles, does not make sense. Here are six reasons you should make the switch to tap water and become part of #TeamTap.

Where does bottled water come from?

This is a secret, hidden from the general public. Although most companies advertise their water as coming from fresh spring water sources, there have been reports of some sneaky companies taking their water straight from the tap! In all honesty, we do not even know what goes into bottled water, as companies are reluctant to tell us.

Does bottled water cost more than tap water?

On the whole, bottled water costs 500–1000 times more than tap water. Furthermore, tap water is so cheap that you could stay hydrated for an entire year for just £1! Does it make sense to spend more money on bottled water, of which the majority could come from your tap in the first place?

> **Did you know?**
>
> *A study in Ireland showed that, even when blindfolded, the majority of people cannot tell the difference between bottled water and tap water by taste. In fact, some research has even shown that people prefer tap water to expensive bottled water.*

Can bottled water be bad for your health?

A recent study showed that 90 per cent of the bottled water we drink contains plastic particles – small bits of plastic which have leached from the bottle into the water over time. What is worse is that we just do not know how long a bottle of water has been sitting in storage. So, it seems that the longer a bottle has been sitting in a warehouse, the higher the concentration of plastic particles there are. Do you like the idea of drinking plastic particles? We do not even know the impact it could have on human health.

Why do people buy bottled water?

Bottled water companies very carefully use phrases such as: 'mineral water', 'river mountain spring water' and 'youthful' to advertise. This can fool consumers into believing their expensive bottled water is better for their health than what they can collect from their own kitchen! In addition, people are so used to the convenience of buying plastic bottles that they don't carry their own water bottles to fill.

What are the health benefits?

There is no evidence that bottled water is even good for you. Frequently, the government checks tap water against stringent rules and regulations. However, bottled water is not checked in the same way. Unbelievably, we don't know how most companies test their water and they may have much lower standards as a result. Surely it is our consumer right to know how they are checking the water? Tap water is well regulated and contains minuscule amounts of necessary chemicals. Chlorine is used in such small amounts that we cannot even tell it is there. It prevents epidemics of diseases such as cholera, dysentery, typhus and hepatitis A.

Conclusion

Bottled water is often drawn from tap water, costs 500–1000 times as much to buy, could be bad for your health, isn't as well regulated as tap water and people can't tell the difference in taste. In comparison, tap water is cheap, healthier, safer and tastes exactly the same.

So, join #TeamTap and help dispense with the overpriced, bottled H_2O.

Lesson 3

This is a repeat of Lesson 2, but using a different word, sentence or grammar focus. A modelled or shared paragraph is written collaboratively and pupils write a paragraph of their own.

Before the lesson, print and copy the example text 'Bottled water: The truth' on pages 38–9 (also available to download from the online resources). Make sure you have one one per pair or small group. You need to decide in advance the word, sentence level or grammar focus for this lesson, based on the list of what is included in the example text.

Introduction (10 mins)

Use the example text 'Bottled water: The truth' as a mini guided-reading exercise: you could ask pupils to read sections independently, read with a partner or read aloud, and you could model reading some sections. Discuss any vocabulary the pupils are unfamiliar with and talk in general terms about the layout of the text.

Main (40 mins)

Find examples in the text (10 mins): Using the example text, look more closely at the word, sentence or grammar focus that you've chosen for the lesson from the list below. Challenge pupils to find as many of them as possible in the text. For example, how many emotive or powerful words, possessive apostrophes and present perfect verbs can you find?

Feature	Simple	Higher level
Generalisers	most, some	the majority, consumers, the general public
Connectives and conjunctions	coordination – and, so subordination – because	furthermore, in addition
Rhetorical question	Do you like the idea of drinking plastic particles?	Surely it is our consumer right to know how they are checking the water?
Verbs	imperatives: join, help	modals: should, could, may
Emotive or powerful vocabulary	terrible, awful	catastrophic, devastating
Punctuation	possessive apostrophe commas to separate items in a list	colon to introduce a list
Tense	present – 'people are'	present perfect – 'there have been'
Description	expanded noun phrases – 'their own kitchen'	expanded noun phrases – 'fresh spring water sources'

Modelled writing (10 mins): Model a short non-chronological report paragraph about one fact from Lesson 1. Include the chosen word, sentence or grammar focus.

Writing (20 mins): Using the word, sentence or grammar focus, pupils write two paragraphs about two different facts from Lesson 1. This works well if you assign two facts to each table. You may want to give different groups different facts so that you have a range of different content for putting together your video by the end of the project.

Plenary (10 mins)

Refocus the pupils on the chosen word, sentence or grammar focus by sharing pupil examples on the board. Ask pupils to show a talk partner where they have successfully used the focus in their own writing, before sharing more examples with the whole class.

Lesson 4

In this lesson, pupils edit their writing, analyse how the example video portrays information to the audience, plan their 'fact scenes' and write an intro and outro.

Introduction (15 mins)

Using talk partners, ask pupils to edit and improve the paragraphs they have written so far in Lessons 2 and 3.

Teaching tip

Ensure that success against the writing foci is recognised, too! You may want to use the school editing policy or provide coloured pens or pencils for children to edit and improve their own and their partner's work.

Main (30 mins)

Take a fact from one of your pupils and write it up on the board. Now, as a whole class, talk about the fact and write up how it might be represented on camera. For example:

- One or more people can narrate the fact part.
- One or more people can be acting out a 'fact scene' at the same time.

Example

Fact: Most people can't tell the difference between tap water and bottled water. Do you think you could honestly taste the difference? Stop wasting your hard-earned money on bottled water!

Fact scene: Two pupils try a blindfolded taste test with one pupil placing the water in front of them to drink. Both testers take off their blindfolds and shrug their shoulders after drinking the water to show that they have no idea which is bottled water and which is tap water.

Plenary (15 mins)

With the help of the whole class, lead writing a collaborative introduction to the video, to be used in the final film. Include a word, sentence or grammar feature from the list of examples from Lessons 2 and 3.

In pairs, children write a short outro for the final video. This could be done in books or on whiteboards using any of the word, sentence or grammar features from the list. Rhetorical questions fit quite nicely into this part, for example, 'Are you one of those crazy people who buys bottled water? Do you want to pay 500 times more than the cost of tap water?'

During or after the lesson, identify which pupils' work will be used for the following parts of the final video:

- intro (shared writing from Lesson 4)
- facts and narrative scenes (writing and ideas from Lessons 2, 3 and 4)
- outro (paired writing from Lesson 4).

Lesson 5

In this lesson, pupils rehearse lines and acting, film their video, watch it back and review it.

Before the lesson, ensure you have decided on which pupils' work will be used for the facts, narrative scenes and outro for the video. It is also helpful if speaking parts have been assigned, your filming device is charged and any props are ready!

Introduction (10 mins)

Watch the example #TeamTap video: www.youtube.com/watch?v=aaXa-piVNfQ. After watching the video, talk about what they like about it, which things they might like to borrow for their own video and which bits they think they would have done differently.

> **Teaching tip**
>
> Remind pupils to keep their scenes short and punchy to keep the audience engaged. Focus on the delivery of the lines to camera in the example video. Making sure their writing is heard clearly on camera is a top priority!

Main (40 mins)

Tell pupils to spend time rehearsing their lines and background narrative scenes, and getting any props ready. It works well if the class is split into groups so that you have a group working on the intro, various groups working on a fact and a final group working on the outro.

Once groups have had enough time, start filming each section.

You may find it easier for editing if the final video is filmed on one device, so you may want to have each group perform in turn once they have all had time to rehearse. Alternatively, you can give each group a device to film with and they can all share their footage with each other using the Cloud or AirPlay. Another alternative is that each group makes their own film with their own intro, facts and outro.

If you decide to film one at a time, involve children as they wait for their turn to film. Roles they can play are:

- director: 'Silence please, camera, action!'
- camera person
- prompter with script.

Plenary (10 mins)

If the final video has all been filmed on one device, it should be quick and easy to watch the whole thing through.

- Review the final film (either as a whole class or in small groups).
- What went well?
- What would they do differently next time?
- How can they now share their film with a wider audience?

For sharing their final film, here are some ideas.

- Share it in a whole-school assembly.
- Send it out to parents via email.
- Include it on the school newsletter using a short URL so that people can find it easily.
- Put it on your school's YouTube account.
- Tweet it out to your wider school community.

Chapter 4
Playful poetry

Introduction

Whilst many people think of 'play' as something children do when they're not learning, mounting research shows that play isn't just a critical component of child development, but also early education. In fact, play is so important to child development that it has been recognised as a Basic Human Right of every child by the United Nations (UN). And yet, despite its importance, it is markedly absent from today's education system.

In this chapter...

In this chapter we will delve deeper into the importance of play in child development and why schools should keep it prevalent in the curriculum throughout a child's educational experiences. This view is endorsed by an interview with Bryn Llewellyn, the co-founder of Tagtiv8, a company that creates 'Physically Active Learning' (PAL) games to integrate into classrooms. We also share Oliver Percovich's story of how he and his skateboard have broken down barriers and provided active and creative learning opportunities for youngsters in Afghanistan, Cambodia and South Africa. Then it will be your turn to discuss and promote play with your children, through the medium of poetry in the six-lesson Why I Play poetry project.

Why is play so important?

Play is about fun, freedom, spontaneity, imagination and creativity. The motivation behind play is play itself. It can have as many or as few rules as you like, exist in set terms or be completely freeform. It's as much about ourselves as it is about the world around us. Play allows children's creativity to flourish, while developing their cognitive and emotional resilience.

From birth onwards, it is through play that children learn to master and engage with the world around them. It allows children to use their imagination to construct a world they feel comfortable in, all the while developing new competencies such as decision-making, teamwork and problem-solving that are needed for successful adult life.

Before they ever step foot into a school hallway, children are learning at a lightning pace. Language, motor skills, emotions, relationships: all of these key skills are explored through play. Before they have even learned how to crawl, infants are able to play with toys, their family and even their voice. Play is, therefore, one of the most important tools in a child's educational toolbox.

Incorporating play into education not only makes the process of learning more enjoyable for pupils, but it encourages them to think about the subject matter on a deeper level. Asking questions, taking chances and embracing uncertainty are just as important in education as they are in play. In fact, when learning is gamified, children have been shown to build more intuitively on skills they've already learned to enhance their game-play.

Playful learning also builds resilience. Rather than causing children stress, play helps children to explore their limitations, take chances and be rewarded with instant feedback. It can be broken into four elements: play, guided play, games and direct instruction.

1. **Play** is when the child has complete control over their activities; it gives them the freedom to do as they wish.

2. **Guided play** is when children are allowed to play under an adult's guidance. Advice, supervision and gentle coaching are incorporated.

3. **Games** are a form of play with rules and guidelines that are designed by an adult. Play is key, but freedom is restricted.

4. **Direct instruction**, unlike the first three, does not involve play. Instead, the activities are designed, controlled and mandated by an adult. The only individual with a sense of agency is the one doing the instructing.

The current education system relies primarily on direct instruction. The result is a rigid learning environment, made up of strict success parameters. Curiosity, confidence and individuality – vital components of education and childhood development – are restricted.

Talking point

When was the last time you created a play experience outside school? Who was involved? How did you come up with the ideas and rules of play?

Play as the foundation for success

Succeeding at school is an important part of being a good student and incorporating play into a child's education can help set them up for success throughout their education pathway. However, there is more at stake in a child's education than their education alone.

When children learn by playing, they learn to love learning. And when a child learns to love learning, they become a student of the world. Their relationships, goals, dreams, values and self-worth all stem from the experiences they go through at an early age. By inspiring a passion for learning and providing pupils with the tools to learn independently, they can provide themselves and others with these kinds of experiences inside and outside of the classroom.

Talking point

Describe a learning experience that you really loved. What made it more enjoyable than other learning experiences?

Play needs to be integrated throughout a child's education and not just preserved for early development. The school systems we currently experience are increasingly more academic and assessment focused. As the children progress on this journey they become more absorbed with compliance than free thought, curiosity and challenge. We need to keep play alive through creative, hands-on and open-ended learning experiences. We need to encourage spontaneity, risk-taking and leading explorations in their learning.

It's easy to forget when talking about children that you are also talking about the person they will become. You're talking about a future parent, an eventual role model; the engineers, artists and leaders of tomorrow are sitting in classrooms today. Teaching them to find comfort within discomfort, to make mistakes, to ask questions and search for answers, to learn from and teach one another through meaningful and positive interactions, will carry them through the rest of their lives. It will nurture a generation of active and engaged citizens. The importance of play is, therefore, of vast and wide-reaching importance, both for individuals and for society at large.

Interview with Bryn Llewellyn

Introducing...

Bryn Llewellyn is an experienced teacher, senior leader and founder of Tagtiv8, a pioneering approach to Physically Active Learning (PAL) and research that not only provides an enjoyable alternative to classroom-based learning, but promotes physical activity – crucial when we all face the increasing problem of sedentary lifestyles.

What's the current problem that you're trying to address?

Ask your children to draw what learning looks like. What will feature? That's right – a teacher at the front of the class with children sat down in rows or at tables, either reading or writing or doing maths. Look closer and many of the images will feature clocks. Why is this? Is it because teachers are always challenging their pupils with pace – 'Come on, you've got five minutes to finish the task.' Or is it because the children are looking at the clock, thinking: 'How long till play time? How long till lunch time? How long till the end of the day?'

Many Western cultures are in the middle of crises – whether these be related to inactivity, obesity and/or mental health. There are more children classified as obese or overweight than ever before. Children are becoming obese earlier and staying obese longer, especially in economically disadvantaged areas. In the past, it was the rich who were large and the poor who were skinny. This scenario is now flipped.

As teachers and leaders, we need to look at ways we can increase and embed creative opportunities for learning. More schools are looking towards PAL as a potential solution to health and education issues. PAL approaches help develop unique and innovative ways to combine English and maths and other curricular areas with physical activity. PAL helps teachers to unlock the potential of the PE hall and outdoor environment for learning core subjects. That said, PAL can also take place in the classroom, not by running around but by using purposeful movement that encourages communication and collaboration.

How can PAL improve performance in the classroom?

Studies show that children who are physically fit are better at absorbing and retaining new information. Research by Dr Andy Daly-Smith at Leeds Beckett University into Tagtiv8 demonstrated impact on levels of physical activity and academic performance. Commenting on the results of the tests, Andy Daly-Smith said: 'The results showed that pupils who took part in a Tagtiv8 lesson achieved over nine minutes more Moderate to Vigorous Physical Activity (MVPA) compared to the traditional classroom lesson and spent 15 minutes less in sedentary time. This contributes towards the 30/30 minutes target for MVPA set out in "Childhood Obesity – a Plan of Action", the government's plan to significantly reduce childhood obesity by supporting healthier choices.'

What are teachers saying about it in the classroom?

The research builds on the observations and anecdotes from teachers with whom I co-deliver PAL sessions. I have lost count of the times teachers say, 'I didn't know he could do that! He's never written it in his maths book or put his hand up in class.'

Yes, there's neuroscience involved, but something special happens when you take the learning outside and/or make it active. PAL approaches engage even the most reluctant of learners, as typified by Kian, a Year 4 pupil from Keighley: 'That game was awesome. It takes a lot to get me to do maths.' According to Bella, a Year 5 pupil from Wakefield: 'With active learning you don't get a chance to get bored... you don't zone out.'

Teachers such as Lianne Collins from Castercliff Academy in Nelson are quick to recognise similar benefits of PAL: 'It helps children overcome their fear of certain subjects.'

What's the simplest way that teachers can get started with this approach to active learning?

Pioneering school leaders such as Ian Holmes from Thorner Primary School in Leeds believe that PAL approaches should not be seen as a gimmick or an add-on. Gone are the days of 'brain breaks'. In his podcast interview with The PE Umbrella, he recognises that 'physical activity should be at the heart of the curriculum'. Children at his school are recognising the rationale and impact of being physically active. It's not a case of running around, getting sweaty and increasing your heart beat. As Jade Morris from Leeds Beckett University says, 'It could be as simple as standing up at the end of a page or a chapter and moving to another part of the classroom to read the next one.'

Atlas of the Future case study: Skate to liberate

Skateistan

On a personal journey to Afghanistan, passionate skateboarder Oliver Percovich found himself 'rolling' the rugged streets of Kabul. Captivated by how children gravitated towards his board when they tried it out, the Australian saw a connection that could help create bonds beyond social barriers. Since there are cultural limits to Afghan girls playing football, riding bicycles or participating in other traditionally male-dominated sports in a society that is rigidly restrictive of women's lives, skateboarding provides a loophole that gives girls a family outside of their homes.

In 2007, Percovich founded Skateistan, a non-profit organisation which uses skateboarding and education for youth empowerment – welcoming students of any ethnicity, gender, religion or social background to their Skate Schools in Afghanistan, Cambodia and South Africa. Today this award-winning organisation runs their programmes, Skate and Create, Back-to-School and Youth Leadership in Kabul,

Mazar-e-Sharif, Phnom Penh, Sihanoukville and Johannesburg. Skateistan reaches over 2,500 youth aged five to 17 every week. Projects include the following.

Outreach

Outreach sessions take place both at the Skate Schools and in the local communities. Educators and Youth Leadership participants head out with skateboards and sports equipment to engage with local children, providing an hour of recreational activity. It is often the first time they will try skateboarding or other sports and their first contact with Skateistan. Skateistan also develops partnerships with child protection agencies in order to connect youth and their families with important social services. Through Outreach sessions, many students go on to register for the Skate and Create or Back-to-School programme.

Skate and Create

This two-hour programme consists of weekly skateboarding classes and an educational arts-based curriculum. In the classroom, Skateistan Educators use creative arts to teach a variety of topics, including human rights, cultural studies, nutrition and the environment. Lessons give youths tools to express themselves, think critically and develop confidence. In the skatepark, students find a valuable platform for self-expression and personal development. Accessible to all levels of literacy and education, Skate and Create provides a safe space for youth to develop friendships that overcome deep social barriers.

Dropping In

The Dropping In programme provides learning spaces and resources where students can develop their aspirations and navigate their potential. Children 'drop in' for organised skateboarding and sports sessions, read in the Skate School libraries, join weekly book clubs and study groups, or use computers and quiet spaces to study. Even when public school is not in session, holiday programmes, field trips, and events keep students learning and moving ahead.

Back to School

Back to School is a programme to support children in their pursuit of formal education. In Afghanistan, this is a fast-tracked learning programme for children who are out of school. Students come to the Skate School five days a week to attend classes covering the national public curriculum. Upon completing the programme, Skateistan enrols students into public school, usually in the third or fourth grade. In South Africa and Cambodia, the programme takes place outside of school hours, where students can 'drop in' and receive homework help and guidance with career and further education planning.

Youth Leadership

Motivated older students at Skateistan can apply to join the Youth Leadership training programme, assisting the Educators in classes, mentoring younger students, building their skill sets and planning local events. This programme helps young people to develop a sense of ownership at the Skate Schools and creates role models for the other students and wider community.

Skateistan runs programmes at their Skate Schools, Outreach locations and with partner organisations in Afghanistan, Cambodia and South Africa. Skateistan Educators run programmes five days a week, reaching more than 2,500 children. 'Skateboarding is now the largest female sport in Afghanistan,' said Percovich in a 2014 TED Talk in Sydney. But skateboarding itself doesn't unlock new opportunities. 'The key is the power of sharing something you love and, with persistence, it can grow into something quite unexpected and truly amazing.'

Discover more online: https://atlasofthefuture.org/project/skateistan

Project 4: Why I play

During this poetry unit, 'Why I Play', you will be exploring two styles of poetry and using pupils' individually written poems to produce a collaborative, filmed final poem.

Lesson 1

In this lesson, you will be exploring poetry and how it works, as well as gathering ideas for the project ahead in terms of content for your own poems about play.

Introduction (10 mins)

As a whole class, discuss the following question: 'What does play mean to you?' Encourage pupils to explore play in all its forms and make notes on the board if you think it will spark good ideas for later.

Main (40 mins)

Part 1 (20 mins): Show the video of Michael Rosen performing his poem 'Gymnastics': www.youtube.com/watch?v=s-9i9Rd1FAE. Discuss the pupils' responses to 'Gymnastics' by first asking them for their immediate response to it. Then, using a large piece of paper, ask each table to work as a group to jot down what the poem makes them think and feel, any questions it might raise and any techniques or vocabulary that stand out for them. You can keep the video playing in the background to allow children to respond to it as it plays. Allow a few minutes for pupils to carousel around other tables to read their ideas.

Next, show the text of the second poem, 'Block City' by Robert Louis Stevenson: https://poets.org/poem/block-city. Allow the pupils a few moments to explore the poem and get to know it by reading it in their heads, before showing the video of Michael Rosen performing it: www.youtube.com/watch?v=Tt6JLQOetew. Repeat the activities above for this second poem. Again, encourage the pupils to carousel around tables to share ideas from other groups.

Part 2 (20 mins): Time to experience play with your class! Organise a mix of physical play and more imaginative play such as creating using paint or blocks, for example, role-playing and drawing. Allow time for the children to properly experience it, and maybe get a little out of breath with the physical side, but the focus is regularly stopping children every few minutes to think about how they feel both physically and emotionally. Encourage them to make notes on mini-whiteboards or paper. Alternatively, use sticky notes ready for sharing in the plenary.

Plenary (10 mins)

Use the IWB or have a flip chart, space on a working wall or large piece of paper, split into two sections: 'Physical' and 'Imaginative'. Give each child two sticky notes, one to jot down how they feel about physical play, and one to note down feelings about imaginative play, for example, 'Running makes me feel free' or 'I lose track of time when I am drawing'. Tell pupils to stick their ideas in the correct section. Choose some ideas to share as a class.

Teaching tip

Throughout the project, it is really helpful if all of the large sheets with shared vocabulary can form a working wall for the children to work from and absorb. This will have a big positive impact on their final work.

Lesson 2

This lesson allows children to explore a free verse poem, before writing and performing collaboratively. Before the lesson, print copies of 'Gymnastics', enough for one per pair. You can find the written version of the poem in Michael Rosen's collection, *Quick, Let's Get Out of Here*. You will also need sets of coloured highlighters, one per table group.

Introduction (5 mins)

Recall and share the ideas the pupils generated in the plenary of Lesson 1, using their reactions to physical play. Inform the children that they are going to explore 'free verse' poetry and what it means.

Teaching tip

Free verse poems have no rhyming structure and often don't have a particular rhythm or syllable patterns; like their name suggests, they are simply 'free'. Free verse, like abstract art, is where the definition of poetry becomes complicated. Reading free verse poetry and discussing why it is a poem, and how where the lines break and the use of longer or shorter lines add to the meaning, can support pupils' understanding. It is very important that children have the opportunity to practise reading these poems aloud using the punctuation and the line breaks to support their reading.

Main (40 mins)

Give out the copies of 'Gymnastics' and tell the pupils to read the poem. Show the performance video from Lesson 1 again if necessary. Tell pupils to work in pairs to find examples of repetition for effect in the poem and to mark the examples with one coloured highlighter (for example, yellow). Discuss as a class. Using different colours for each technique, repeat this activity to highlight examples of:

- word choice to create mood
- rhythm and varying sentence length
- onomatopoeia.

For each poetic technique, have a quick discussion about the impact on the reader and what implication the technique has for performing the poem to an audience. Next, using mini-whiteboards or tablets, encourage pupils to create their own short poems, similar to 'Gymnastics'. Within each table group, children split into pairs and decide on one of the poetic devices:

- repetition for effect
- word choice to create mood
- rhythm and varying sentence length
- onomatopoeia.

(It doesn't matter at this stage if not all devices are used across each table group, as long as each pair within the group chooses a different device.)

Each pair within the group writes a few lines of free verse poetry, relating to how they play, and focusing on physical reactions to play. They then decide on an order for their work to create a collaborative, group poem.

Plenary (15 mins)

Pupils have a few minutes within each group to rehearse performing their poem. They might choose to read a line each, read the lines they wrote with their partner or read the whole poem as a group. Ask them to suggest what makes a powerful performance before they start.

Finally, ask the groups to perform their free verse poems for the class. Reflect on their success – what worked and what did not?

Lesson 3

This lesson uses the same format as Lesson 2, to allow children to explore a rhyming poem, before writing and performing collaboratively. Before the lesson, print copies of 'Block City', enough for one per pair: https://poets.org/poem/block-city. You also need a set of coloured highlighters, one per table group.

Introduction (5 mins)

Recall and share the ideas the children generated in the plenary of Lesson 1, this time concentrating on their reactions to imaginative play. Introduce the idea of rhyming poetry and a rhyme scheme.

Teaching tip

A rhyme scheme is the pattern of rhymes at the end of each line of a poem or song. It is usually referred to by using letters to indicate which lines rhyme; lines designated with the same letter all rhyme with each other.

Main (40 mins)

Give out copies of 'Block City' by Robert Louis Stevenson and tell the pupils to read it. Show the performance video from Lesson 1 again if necessary.

As in Lesson 2, tell pupils to work in pairs to find examples of rhyme in the poem and to mark the examples with one coloured highlighter (for example, pink).

As a class, discuss how this poem is different to the free verse poem 'Gymnastics', shared in Lesson 2. Can the pupils identify the rhyming pattern? (AA, BB, CC) Do rhymes have to always be 'perfect' rhymes, or can some be a little more tenuous? Do the pupils think this matters? Using different-coloured highlighters for each technique, tell pupils to work in pairs to label examples of:

- metaphor (let the sofa be mountains)
- alliteration (song of sailors, I saw it I see it)
- imaginative description
- use of synonym.

Next, encourage pupils to write short poems, similar to 'Block City'. Within each table group, children split into pairs and decide on one of the poetic devices to focus on:

- metaphor (let the sofa be mountains)
- alliteration (song of sailors, I saw it I see it)
- imaginative description
- use of synonym.

Tell each pair to write a rhyming couplet relating to a type of imaginative play, focusing on how it makes them feel. Then, in their group, tell them to decide on an order for their work to create a collaborative, group poem.

Plenary (15 mins)

Give pupils a few minutes within each group to rehearse performing their poem. They might choose to read a line each, read the lines they wrote with their partner or read the whole poem as a group. Table groups perform their rhyming poems for the class. Reflect on their success – what worked and what didn't?

Finally, as a class, decide which style of poem they would like to produce for their collaborative final piece. There are no rules so even a mix of the two is a good choice.

Lesson 4

In this lesson, the class work together to write a shared opening for a poem, before pupils plan their own writing.

Introduction (5 mins)

By this point, you need to have decided whether to collaborate on a rhyming or a free verse style poem. As a class, discuss which style you have chosen and what that means for the structure of your poem.

Main (45 mins)

Part 1 (15 mins): Use a whole-class shared write to produce the opening lines for your class poem, using either the structure of 'Block City' (AA BB CC) or free verse as in 'Gymnastics'. This should be a generic opening about play, which will allow pupils to add their own ideas about play to the final videoed poem. The example lines below are taken from 'Block City'.

Example

Let the sofa be mountains, the carpet be sea,
There I'll establish a city for me:
A kirk and a mill and a palace beside,
And a harbor as well where my vessels may ride.

Throughout this shared writing, encourage pupils to verbalise their thought processes, selecting and improving vocabulary, commenting on poetic devices, and re-reading what has already been written. You could have pupils sharing ideas on mini-whiteboards or orally.

Remind the pupils of the ideas and vocabulary you shared earlier in the project, focusing on their ideas of play, and their emotional and physical responses to it.

Part 2 (30 mins): Tell children to work individually to plan and draft their own poem, based on your chosen structure. It is really useful to display the notes that you have built up so far in these lessons to help pupils develop their ideas.

Extension challenge: Ask children to rewrite some of their poem, based on the alternative structure that you could have chosen (for example, if they wrote a free verse poem, get them to write a rhyming poem).

Plenary (10 mins)

Ask pupils to work with talk partners and explain their ideas for their poems. Talk partners comment back to the class on what they liked about their partner's ideas.

Allow a few minutes at the end of the lesson for children to add any ideas they like to their own planning sheets.

After the lesson: You may want to have the shared opening from Lesson 4 typed or written up on slips to stick in books as an opening to the writing in the next lesson. Otherwise, make sure you save it so the pupils can use it in their written work in Lesson 5.

Lesson 5

In this lesson, pupils work independently, using the shared writing and their own planning from Lesson 4 to write their own poems.

> **Teaching tip**
>
> You may want to have the shared writing opening from Lesson 4 typed or written up on slips to stick in books as an opening to the writing in this lesson.

Introduction (10 mins)

Display the shared writing opening from Lesson 4 and remind the children of different poetic devices they can use within their own writing. Talk through any that they don't fully understand:

- metaphor
- alliteration
- imaginative description
- synonyms
- repetition
- onomatopoeia
- word choice to create a mood
- rhythm and varied sentence length.

Main (35 mins)

Tell pupils to write and edit their own poems. They do not need to write new opening lines to the poem as they will use the shared writing for this. As pupils write, you may wish to draw together a focus group, or run mini-plenaries allowing children to share successes, ask for help with ideas and rhymes, or address any misconceptions.

Plenary (15 mins)

Ask pupils to choose lines from their work to be used for the final, collaborative class poem. Limit groups to a few lines each to keep the collaborative poem a reasonable length! You can type these up on the board as you invite groups to share their work. Ask for live feedback to improve them if necessary.

Lesson 6

In this lesson, the collaborative class poem is rehearsed, performed and recorded.

Introduction (10 mins)

Watch one or two of Michael Rosen's poetry performance videos: www.youtube. com/channel/UC7D-mXO4kk-XWvH6lBXdrPw. Discuss how he uses his voice, face and body to perform poems. Note down on the board a checklist of ways to make a performance interesting.

Main (40 mins)

Rehearse the opening lines (10 mins): It can work well to have the first shared lines of the poem read chorally by the whole class or a group. This allows you to rehearse performing this as a group, focusing on performing cohesively, using the same intonation and expression.

Group rehearsals (10 mins): Then get children to spend time rehearsing a section of the poem in their groups. Encourage everyone to have a line or half a line each and work on delivering them in one seamless flow. Keep the pupils working in groups to give each other feedback on performance using the checklist from the introduction. Facial expression will add to the expression and intonation the audience will hear.

Record the poem (20 mins): Record each line from the collaborative poem using either the voice-over function on Adobe Spark Video or by recording the pupils performing as a video.

Teaching tip

Doing a mix of video and voice-over helps you to include pupils who don't feel so confident on camera and keeps the viewer interested with a mix of styles. You could get footage of the children playing at breaktime or during PE and use that for your voice-over sections. This really makes the video come alive!

Plenary (10 mins)

Once you've recorded the whole poem, use the Adobe Spark Video free photo library to add visual interest to your voice-over sections. If you can, do this as a whole class on the board by:

- plugging in your tablet using an HDMI/VGA adaptor
- AirPlaying your tablet
- logging into spark.adobe.com and using the desktop version to finish off the video.

Chapter 5
Roving reporters

Introduction

Should we encourage our children to read the news? This is a question that generates a great deal of discussion amongst teachers and parents. There are those who feel it is imperative that children grow up understanding the realities of life and what goes on around them and in the world. Then there are those who wish to protect children from what are most often upsetting, horrific or damaging stories. However, there is a happy medium in exposing children to the news that is tailored in appropriate ways for their growing minds and maturity. Great examples of this can be found through media such as *The Week Junior* magazine and CBBC's *Newsround*.

In this chapter...

In this chapter we will consider the importance of including news in a child's education and hear from a journalistic writer and editor on her perspectives. Susanna Rustin, Feature Writer and Editor at the *Guardian*, shares her thoughts on engaging young people in the news and how having a news-literate population would be of great benefit for everyone. In our case study, we hear more about the work of Atlas of the Future themselves and how they shine a light on projects that aim to solve the challenges of today and tomorrow. Then it's time to inspire the next generation of authentic news reporters in creating their own reliable news pieces using the six-lesson Roving Reporters project.

Why share the news?

It is every parent's goal to prepare their children for the world as they grow in age, independence and understanding. Each experience along the way provides opportunities for learning. However, some parents choose to try and intervene or intercept those learning experiences in a bid to protect their child. But is this ultimately helping them prepare fully for their futures? How will they learn if they don't make mistakes? How will they develop resilience and learn to think critically and strategically in the face of problem-solving? How will they build emotional resilience if they are not exposed to information that they can grapple with and question?

Protecting our children from all potential challenges, difficulties and realities they face will surely only reduce their capacity to flourish and fully succeed in the ever-changing world that they are growing up in. We need to ensure that both at home and in school, we provide the 'safe' way to experience these realities through well-planned, educational activities and discussions. We want children to be curious about life. We need them to be interested in and empathetic about the world we live in and how it differs from the world they know. Providing opportunities like these will help shape the next generation in global awareness whilst developing their own emotional skills and coping mechanisms.

Children have a habit of inadvertently picking up what's in the news, perhaps from their phone, the radio in the car, a newspaper headline in a shop, or from their peers at school. Hearing snippets of information, or misunderstanding meanings of words, can lead children to form overstated worries about what they have picked up. We understand that very often the news can seem scary for children and that it is a parent's instinct to want to steer the child away from anything that might upset them. However, we have a responsibility to help children become more aware of events from around the world, the same world in which they will become adults, fending for themselves. It is essential that the information the children receive comes from reliable sources and through age-appropriate resources and discussions. They need to understand that the source of information must be independent, adequately researched and balanced.

Talking point

When did you last read, watch or listen to the news? In what format did you read, watch or listen to it? Did you discuss it with anyone? Did it create questions in your head?

The rise of fake news

The term 'fake news' became commonplace in no small part thanks to President Donald Trump, who coined it to describe stories and publicists he deemed to be unscrupulous. More often than not, though, he used the term to discredit anything that criticised him, or that he simply did not agree with. The concept of 'fake news' has since grown to encompass any story that is presented as truth, but has very little – if any – grounding in fact at all.

Share with the class

As a phenomenon, fake news is not so new. The practice of writing bogus stories to get attention has been around for centuries, dating as far back as the 17th century with reports of monsters on the loose with 'goat's legs, a human body, seven arms and seven heads', or stories of a woman surviving for 14 years without eating or drinking anything (*1843 Magazine*, 2017).

Fake news still existed even during the golden age of journalism in the 19th and 20th centuries. We called it propaganda and it was a powerful political tool that caused plenty of problems in its wake.

Early in the 21st century though, the propaganda paradigm shifted. This time, social media was the disruptor, and it changed the way that people consumed news so drastically, that fake news was able to thrive.

The same rules as the old propaganda days still holds true: by presenting someone with information that reinforces their preconceived world view, particularly if that individual feels marginalised or persecuted by a group or state, you can influence and shape their opinions.

Whereas in previous decades, newspapers have only been able to distribute one set of stories to their readership each day, now it's possible to flood news channels with millions of pieces of content, and to uniquely distribute each of them to people based on their behaviours and belief systems.

The effect of fake news on youth

Typically, children have been sheltered from mass media. Only when they became of reading age – or joined their family to watch the evening news – were they able to consume stories of the world around them. The accessibility of social media, however, has changed that entirely.

Now, media outlets are able to push news stories to children wherever they are online. A report by Common Sense Media, published in 2015, showed that teenagers spend on average two hours per day on social media, making them more and more susceptible to the effects of (dis-)information overload.

Share with the class

The effects of fake news are already being felt by many children, as demonstrated by a 2018 study carried out by the National Literacy Trust. The study was called 'Fake news and critical literacy', and it surveyed 2,000 children between the ages of 8–16, asking them to examine six news stories and determine which were true and which were 'fake news'. Three of the reports were genuine and the other three were bogus.

The results spoke volumes both in terms of the children's ability to think critically about what they were reading and the convincingness of some of the fake news stories that are being churned out. In fact, just two per cent of children were able to correctly identify all six stories as either genuine or fake (Education Executive, 2018). Following the results, the children were asked how they felt about their ability to spot fake news. Perhaps unsurprisingly, over half of them admitted to being concerned that they were not able to spot fake news reliably enough. Fake news has also been raised as a concern by MPs due to the adverse effect it can have on children's self-esteem and trust. On many occasions, children have reported that they suffered anxiety and embarrassment after sharing fake news stories that they thought were real (BBC, 2018).

Talking point

How do we know if something is fake news? What are the issues in accepting all news as real?

Who is responsible for protecting children from fake news?

The question of who should take the lead in supporting young people to think critically about the media they consume is a difficult one.

Andreas Schleicher, Director of Education and Skills for the Organisation for Economic Co-operation and Development (OECD), wrote in 2017 that pupils need to be taught the necessary skills to allow them to spot fake news while they are in school. 'One lesson devoted to critical thinking is not enough [...] rather critical thinking should be weaved throughout the entire curriculum.' His hope is that this will help to reduce the 'echo-chamber' effect that social media creates.

There is a high degree of responsibility being placed on schools and teachers here, something that Geoff Barton of the Association of School and College Leaders recognised when he said that schools are 'on the front line of trying to provide a solution to a society-wide issue' (BBC, 2018).

Teachers seem to agree that they should bear this responsibility, with 98.8 per cent of those who were interviewed by the National Literacy Trust agreeing. Over

50 per cent of the same group said that they believe the current curriculum falls short of actually fulfilling this responsibility (Education Executive, 2018).

There are resources and advice for parents who want to help their children to be vigilant about the content they pay attention to online. Nicky Cox, who edits a paper called *First News*, a newspaper specifically aimed at children, provides some guidance on the type of questions parents should encourage their children to ask themselves about stories they read online. These include: 'Do other sites have the same facts and figures?', 'Has it been reported on the radio, TV and in more than one reputable newspaper?' and 'Is some of the text written in caps – usually a sign of sensationalism – or [with] lots of exclamation marks?'

One possible issue with this is that parents may be as inept at spotting fake news as their children, or perhaps they are aware that some of the stories they are sharing are sensationalist and exaggerated and they do it anyway (Information Literacy Group, 2018).

Interview with Susanna Rustin

Introducing...

Susanna Rustin is a journalist at the *Guardian*, and previously worked at the *Financial Times*. She is currently a lead writer on social affairs, and has also worked as an editor on the Opinion and Review sections. She is a local campaigner and community councillor.

Why should children study the news?

There's the form of the news and the content of the news and I think children should study both of them. For younger children, teaching the content requires sensitivity because much of the content can be pretty negative. Children are very conscious of the shadow that things like Brexit casts. There are lots of touch points but they don't necessarily understand them. Unfortunately, the UK curriculum is quite poor on current affairs unlike the US, which, from personal experience, is quite hot on it.

On the subject of shying away from violent crime, violence and war – I'm not necessarily advocating a hugely up-to-the-minute news curriculum but, if the point of school is to train a child up to be an adult in the world, to learn to understand the world and their place in it, then they need to be exposed to a broader range of current affairs before they are squeezed into a specialism.

What has changed to make studying the news so important these days?

Children absolutely need the skills to critically examine information and ideas about the world that mainstream media tends to focus on (crime, immigration and so on) and also understanding what the BBC is about, how it's funded, how Murdoch media is funded and some critical thinking about different news sources. They should look at the difference between news and comment and adverts because increasingly social media is giving news at scale and speed but it's not necessarily reliable. Our contemporary institutions aren't very well represented in the curriculum compared to the amount of time they spend studying kings and queens. Which one will serve them more now?

How do we get young people interested in the news rather than or at least as much as they are interested in celebrity culture?

The climate strikes are a brilliant way of getting them involved. I never used to think that the voting age should be lowered but now I definitely agree that it should be lowered to 16, perhaps earlier. We place importance on money, literacy and numeracy, social skills, turning up on time, all those things that we do in schools to prepare children for adult life and yet we don't teach them politics. I'm sure there's a lot of suspicion that teachers are very lefty and so it wouldn't be perhaps so balanced but that's why you have a curriculum. I think you'd have some fascinating discussions in class, especially in multicultural classrooms where other countries' news is just as important.

The other way to get children into the news is through sport and music and then using that to slide into geography, history and current affairs or by starting locally and building up to looking nationally.

What effect would having a fully news-literate population have on wider society?

Having a more news-literate society would make society more rational. Right now, I don't think people are rational at all and they think that certain things are way more common than they actually are (immigration, abduction). News values distort our perception of reality, and understanding the *Sun* newspaper and where its news comes from can give us a much more balanced political view. When people are asked to estimate crime or migrants in their area or where they fit on the income scale, it shows that people need education and years of effort to fully understand their place in the world and what the world actually is like.

Climate change in particular cannot be overestimated as a challenge for this generation of children, one that the adult generation hasn't risen to. News literacy will help to prepare them to take it seriously. Childhood should be a protected space so news has to be mediated and approached sensibly. We haven't done a great job of it up to now so we can't do much worse than to just have a go!

Atlas of the Future case study: Atlas of the Future

Cathy Runciman is the co-founder of Atlas of the Future, an online storytelling platform that shines a light on people and their projects aiming to solve the challenges we face today and tomorrow, across all areas of human activity. She divides her time with another non-profit global media platform – openDemocracy – leading on partnerships and strategy. In a previous life, Cathy worked for 12 years as Managing Director for *Time Out International*, launching print and digital media businesses. She is also an advisor to the board of Makerversity, is a governor for the Goldsmiths Press, and runs an annual magazine publishing project at a local school. Here she tells us more about the Atlas of the Future project.

We started Atlas of the Future to celebrate and raise the profile of people working to solve the many challenges we all face. We hoped to give space to people who dedicate their talents to a better tomorrow, people with a long-term vision for better futures. We wanted to counter the short-termism and fear-fuelled narratives that were present in many media by telling diverse stories of hope and creativity – from every part of the world and across every area of human activity.

We hoped that if we could uncover and tell such stories, week in and week out, that this might light a spark of joy and possibility in others. By 'speaking human' and putting people first – working with them so that they can tell their stories in an accessible and entertaining way – we want to break down barriers of culture, language, age and experience. We hope to encourage people to take part in shaping a fairer and more sustainable future that will truly benefit everyone, everywhere. We call this mission 'democratising the future'.

We know from the people we feature on the Atlas that they face many challenges – often struggling for years with infrastructure, communications or the finance needed for their projects to be sustainable in the long term or be able to grow. By providing a platform for their work, by always inviting them to include a call to action, and by connecting people together at our events such as Fixing the Future, we hope to support their efforts. Sharing their stories, making connections to other people and projects, working, learning and listening collectively and collaboratively is part of the work we do to make these ideas more mainstream.

We think of ourselves as critical, cautious optimists. When you spend each day talking to wonderful people who are completely committed to future generations, people who put the earth first, people who care about being good ancestors, it's hard not to be filled with hope, in spite of the very many and serious problems we face. There are stories of great hardship but also great joy – and joy is a vital part of the work we do, and an essential element of the future we want to be part of.

Project 5: Plastic Times

Over the next six lessons, pupils will be writing a newspaper report using a CNN documentary for inspiration.

Lesson 1

In this lesson, pupils watch a CNN documentary and gather information to write a newspaper report.

Introduction (15 mins)

Give each pupil a mini-whiteboard or a piece of paper with the 5Ws on:

- What?
- Where?
- When?
- Why?
- Who?

Start a whole-class discussion about plastic pollution. What do they know about it? Use the 5Ws as a way to frame your discussion. Encourage pupils to make their own notes and share them with the rest of the class.

Main (30 mins)

Next, watch the 14-minute documentary on Midway Island from CNN to get a more up-close-and-personal perspective on plastic pollution: https://edition.cnn.com/videos/us/2016/11/30/midway-plastic-island-nick-paton-walsh-orig-jql.cnn

---

Teaching tip

The documentary states 'viewer discretion is advised'; six minutes in it shows a dead bird being opened up to reveal the plastic it has eaten. I recommend you watch this beforehand just to ease your mind, but it is fairly tame and the rest of the video is totally fine for young viewers.

Discuss pupils' reaction to the documentary. Then, ask them to revisit the 5Ws in groups and make notes on each section about the content of the video they have just watched.

Plenary (15 mins)

Lead a whole-class discussion allowing pupils to share their reactions to the documentary in the context of the 5Ws. Take notes at the front of the class to be used in later lessons.

Lesson 2

In this lesson, pupils will use the 5Ws notes from Lesson 1 to write an overview section for their newspaper article. Before the lesson, find a newspaper article online. It doesn't have to be related to plastic pollution, but should clearly show the structural features of a newspaper article as listed in the introduction to the lesson.

Introduction (15 mins)

Display the newspaper article you've chosen. As a class, discuss the structure of a newspaper article using visual clues from the online article. Can you identify the following?

- headline
- strapline
- overview section
- detailed section
- interview
- summary or conclusion.

Tell pupils to work in pairs and have a go at writing a headline and a strapline using the Midway Island video as the context. Share examples as a whole class, identify good examples and how to improve them by modelling on the board.

Main (35 mins)

Talk about how to write an overview of a story. How much should you say? What details should you give? What must you leave the viewer wanting to do? Using the 5Ws notes from Lesson 1, discuss how you might use that information to write an overview section for your article. What should an overview of the story include? How much detail should it have? Then ask your pupils to have a go at writing an overview.

This is a good time for you to introduce a sentence level focus for their writing, for example, fronted adverbials or whatever your current sentence level focus is.

Example

Recently, President Obama visited the island.

Plenary (10 mins)

Finally, ask partners to work together to peer-edit their overviews to check that they make sense and contain examples of appropriate sentence level work. Get pupils to read out good examples of work to the rest of the class, focusing on their presentation skills in preparation for filming their work at the end of the project.

Lesson 3

In this lesson, pupils write the detail section of their news report article.

Introduction (20 mins)

This lesson is about drilling down into the details. First, rewatch the section of the Midway Island documentary where they cut open the bird's stomach (5:39–7:16). Next, ask what effect the report is trying to create by going into detail. Lead your pupils to understand that, by giving the gruesome details, the reader will understand just how big the plastic problem is.

Make notes on the board, perhaps using a food chain diagram, to demonstrate that there is a direct link between birds eating plastic to us as humans eating plastic. Present the information really clearly so that children can use it to write a detailed section for their news article. Verbally share ideas for fronted adverbials using the IWB file:

- a time-based fronted adverbial – Earlier today
- an action-based fronted adverbial – As quickly as possible
- an opinion-based fronted adverbial – Disappointingly.

Main (30 mins)

Now tell pupils to write a detailed section for their news article using the notes on the board and sentence level work to help structure their writing. Take regular breaks in order to share examples of sentence level work.

Plenary (10 mins)

Tell partners to work together to peer-edit their work, checking that it makes sense and contains examples of appropriate sentence level work. Get pupils to read out good examples of work to the rest of the class, focusing on presentation skills in preparation for filming their work at the end of this project.

Lesson 4

In this lesson, pupils write the interview section for their news article.

Introduction (20 mins)

Discuss the following questions as a whole class.

- What is an interview for?
- Who would you ask to do an interview?
- What kind of things would you ask?

Stage a mock interview with a willing pupil at the front of the class. Ask open and closed questions to show the difference between questions that encourage interviewees to share details (open) and ones that only require a yes or no answer (closed). Discuss the difference between these styles of questions.

As a whole class, come up with questions you would ask US Marine National Monuments Superintendent Matt Brown from the Midway Island video and write them on the IWB file. The pupils will pick from these questions and write answers to them in the main section of this lesson. Next, talk about how you would introduce these questions in the article.

Example

We asked Midway Island wildlife expert, Matt Brown, how he thought life had changed on the island. 'In the last five years, I have seen more and more birds suffer from eating plastic which they mistake for fish. It's a really sad situation, so much worse than it looks on television.'

Main (30 mins)

In pairs, tell pupils to choose from the questions and write the answers to them. Include sentence level work here, specifically direct and indirect (reported) speech.

Using direct speech only for the answers makes things easier to write. This is a perfect opportunity to look at writing responses using indirect speech with higher-ability children.

Example

Next, we began talking about what he thought would happen to the island if the situation carried on. He replied by saying that he thought that the island's remaining 60 inhabitants would probably have to leave if the situation got much worse, making the island into a ghost town.

Hold regular mini-plenaries to share examples of how pupils are recording their answers.

Plenary (10 mins)

Pick a question from the shared list and pick a pupil from each group to answer that question by reading their response out to the rest of the group. Then get pupils to read out good examples of work to the rest of the class, focusing on presentation skills in preparation for filming their work at the end of this project. Be sure to invite a response written using indirect (reported) speech.

Lesson 5

In this lesson, pupils write a conclusion for their news article. Before the lesson, find a newspaper article online. It doesn't have to be related to plastic pollution, but should clearly show a summary and opinion.

Introduction (15 mins)

Watch the conclusion to the CNN video, from 13:20 until the end. How does the journalist close the report? Display the example newspaper article to identify some closing features from the CNN report, like summary and opinion.

Explain to pupils that a summary should remind the audience of the main message of the article. It should also mention anything the audience should do now they have read it – 'a call to action'. Opinions should be saved until the end of an article so the audience has all the facts first. Giving your own opinions helps the audience understand what you think about the issue and helps them form their own opinion.

Make notes on the board using ideas from the class about how they might close their own news reports. This is a good time to gather useful vocabulary, calls to action and any sentence level work that you want pupils to use.

Main (35 mins)

Tell pupils to work in pairs to write a concluding paragraph for their newspaper article using some of the notes from the introduction. Take regular breaks to share examples of good work and sentence level work. Whole-class sentence level work could be about using opinion sentence starters. Rhetorical questions could be used to extend higher-ability pupils.

Example

It's easy to see why…
It seems to me that…
I strongly oppose...

Isn't it time we started taking this issue more seriously?

Plenary (10 mins)

Tell pupils to peer-edit their work in pairs, focusing on sentence level work. Then, get pupils to read out good examples of work to the rest of the class, focusing on presentation skills in preparation for filming their work at the end of this project.

Lesson 6

In this lesson, pupils will use all the work they have done in the previous five lessons to film their own news report.

Introduction (20 mins)

Summarise the sections of a news report that pupils have written:

- headline and strapline
- overview section
- detailed section
- interview
- summary or conclusion.

As a whole class, work together to write an intro and outro to the news report that pairs or groups can use to start and end their filming.

Teaching tip

It might be useful to use YouTube to explore how news reports start and end.

Example

Intro: Welcome to Class 5R News at seven o'clock. Tonight, we bring you a special news report which some viewers might find shocking…

Outro: That's all from us at Class 5R News. Thanks for watching and remember, stay safe and pick up your plastic. Goodnight!

Use the remaining introduction time to model how to film a section of their work using something like Adobe Spark Video. Review the following techniques:

- filming to camera
- using images and voice-over
- including text to emphasise key points.

Main (30 mins)

Give groups time to film their work. See if they can use a mix of styles from the bullet points above to make their news report more varied and interesting. If some pupils have written huge amounts in some sections, challenge them to pick out five key sentences that can be filmed in a short amount of time.

Plenary (10 mins)

Share examples of good videos on the board or ask groups to swap tablets or laptops so that they can see each other's work. If groups have only had time to film their work, you could use an ICT lesson to edit their news reports using Adobe Spark Video.

Chapter 6
Greta the Great

Introduction

Thinking back to Chapter 1, another poignant example of pupil politics comes from Sweden. Teenager Greta Thunberg is a climate change activist, and has seated herself firmly at the table of the global debate. Amongst her impressive list of achievements is holding meetings with the UN Secretary General.

So, how did she succeed where so many large organisations have failed?

She started small.

Thunberg began with a simple solo strike from school to protest climate change and has now inspired school strikes in more than 270 cities all over the world, from Europe and the US to Australia and Japan. More than 20,000 students have been involved in these strikes, proving that young people today are deeply invested not only in politics, but also in all social and environmental issues. Thunberg seems to be echoing Michelle Obama's messaging (see page 4) when she says that, 'Since our leaders are behaving like children, we will have to take the responsibility they should have taken long ago.'

Of all the things we teach, lessons about the environment are perhaps the most important. The planet is changing fast and our own activities are driving that change.

Talking point

What do you know about Greta Thunberg? Have you, or anyone you know, been involved in a climate change strike? What do you think about this approach to raising awareness about climate change?

In this chapter...

In this chapter we will look into the dilemma of a growing economy and a depleting environment and how it can be approached positively through environment storytelling. Neil Roskilly, Chief Executive of the Independent Schools' Association (ISA), shares his views on whether children should be exposed to global issues and we hear about the ambitious and inspiring African-led initiative 'The Great Green Wall', that aims to grow an 8,000 km new wonder of the world across the entire width of the continent. Then turn to the five-lesson Greta the Great project to transform your pupils into the next leaders of climate change, as they create their own series of powerful speeches and videos in support of the cause.

The battle between the environment and the economy

The issues of climate change and the decline of natural species are closely intertwined in a vicious circle of cause and effect. As industrial activities involving the burning of fossil fuels release carbon dioxide into the atmosphere, they drive climate change. The same activities also tend to destroy wildlife habitats, driving declines in many animal species. The resulting reduction in biodiversity makes us more vulnerable to the effects of climate change, by reducing the adaptability of our living world. And climate change is further worsened by the loss of plant life, which reduces carbon storage. It's a cycle of destruction fuelling destruction.

Environmental conservation and a growing economy do not sit easily together. One tends to make the other worse in the short term.

Prosperous societies are often the ones having the most negative environmental impacts. In fact, the better an economy performs, the more carbon dioxide is released into our atmosphere. This happens because economies are driven by often environmentally destructive industries and practices. Well-paid citizens tend to drive long miles to work and fly abroad on holiday. Successful employers may also fly their staff to conferences and training sessions, while a lot of energy is used to heat and ventilate busy workplaces.

So, is a thriving economy incompatible with a healthy environment? After all, in the short term, environmental legislation has the potential to drastically reduce the profitability and scale of businesses.

In reality though, we ask ourselves a different question: are we willing to let a thriving economy come at the expense of safeguarding life on earth?

Share with the class

Broadcaster and natural historian Sir David Attenborough expressed this eloquently, in conversation with the Duke of Cambridge in January 2019:

'Every breath of air we take, every mouthful of food that we take comes from the natural world… If we damage the natural world, we damage ourselves. We are one, coherent ecosystem.' (www.youtube.com/watch?v=9W6NxE6A paw&feature=youtu.be)

Shifting the narrative of environment storytelling

It's not uncommon for us to feel despairing about our future on Earth. Things can appear so bleak that we can't imagine that there is any hope of fixing them. Attitudes like this can become a habitual response to continual bad news about the environment. In fact, researcher Denise Baden is concerned that this passive fatalism may prevent us from taking positive steps to improve matters.

She asks whether our perceptions are worsened by the plethora of possible dystopian futures presented in cinema, television and literature, citing the *Black Mirror* television series as a powerful example of a source of cautionary tales about the future, which can make us feel anxious and pessimistic (Baden, 2018).

Instead, Baden recommends that we combat fatalism in our attitudes to environmental issues, by changing our narratives and creating the opportunity for positive outcomes to be visualised and actively pursued.

As an antidote to dominant tales about dystopian futures, the Green Stories project run by the University of Southampton invites writers to create stories which depict the future of the environment in a positive light. In 2018, the project ran a short story competition.

The truth is: we can all change the stories that we tell.

While teaching about the serious nature of the challenges we face, we can also choose to focus on the environmental actions which have the potential to change our course. We can engage learners in understanding the amazing things that people have done, and imagining what we may yet achieve.

Talking point

In what ways could you raise awareness about an environmental issue? What suggestions do you have for tackling climate change?

This positive, 'dare-to-dream' mindset is how innovators have conjured up environment-changing technologies that have the power to shape the world we live in for the better. A whole genre of technology has emerged in recent years with the explicit intention of saving the environment. It's a phenomenon that eco-innovation researcher René Kemp has termed a kind of 'relative decoupling' – whereby economic growth is becoming less environmentally damaging.

Young people care about climate change and the future of our planet, perhaps because it affects them most of all. Many take individual actions such as using active transport and recycling their waste. They may also become involved in advocacy and activism, as nine students from Melbourne University did when they stood on the roof of the campus's old quad building and stripped off their clothes to reveal the message 'drop your assets' painted on their skin. The group were protesting the university's investment in the fossil fuel industry, part of a national day of student climate action (Press, 2018).

Examples like this demonstrate the passion and creativity inherent in human nature, which may yet change the way we live on our planet.

Environmental storytelling can promote this passion. We must provide young people with the knowledge they need to understand what is important in the environment and what we need to change. More importantly perhaps, we must also inspire them to believe that change is possible. It is only by insisting on this shift in environment storytelling that we can reverse the tide of fatalistic attitudes towards our ability to actually contribute meaningful change.

Interview with Neil Roskilly

Introducing...

Neil Roskilly is Chief Executive of the Independent Schools Association (ISA), the charity and membership association that represents 535+ schools, 11,000 teachers and 116,000 pupils in the UK. His 36-year career in education includes headship and teaching in both the state and independent sectors, as well as international and extensive governance experience. Neil advises UK regulators and a range of examination awarding bodies at the policy level.

Do you think children should be exposed to global issues?

Parents are fighting a battle because, through tech, children are being exposed to global news and events in a way that has never happened before. News is more graphic – there's a much greater variety of sources and not all of them are reliable, of course. Many see this exposure as a loss of childhood itself, but it's almost impossible and not always desirable to insulate children from the issues that now surround them. Perhaps this is a good thing, though children need to be taught the coping skills and strategies that will help them to make sense of an increasingly complex world. Schools have an important part to play here, just as parents do, in helping children acclimatise and develop an understanding of the issues that affect their lives. It helps that children on the whole are passionate and concerned global citizens, perhaps more so than any previous generation. Any open and democratic society wants its citizens to be politically aware and engaged in the decision-making process at a local and national level. Isolating children from the events around them will only lead to disenfranchisement and a sense of helplessness.

As just one example, the recent school climate strikes, whatever your view, enable children to develop their thinking to a deeper level, through debate and research. Schools should grasp such opportunities when they arise. Even when a school's faith, custom and values are seemingly opposed to an issue such as equality, those values can be strengthened through debate. They won't be strengthened through deeper isolation. Children upon leaving school can struggle in an open society if they have little understanding of that society. A top grade means very little if a school has not equipped children to cope with the increasingly complex pressures of the real world.

Whatever approach a school takes, perhaps its most important task is to instil hope. Hope in the future and hope in being able to face its pressures. If a child feels lost and isolated, no number of qualifications or certificates will create a fulfilling and meaningful life.

What would be your preferred approach to the curriculum?

At primary level, successful schools take a topic-based or thematic approach to learning where subjects are less defined. This encourages children to practise a range of transferable skills from different areas of experience. Given the low starting point for many, it's no surprise that their rates of progress during this primary phase is often much more marked than at secondary level where the curriculum is usually more compartmentalised. In secondary, unless the curriculum is carefully mapped and cross-pollination encouraged, pupils are rarely asked to apply their skills and understanding across the subjects. There are perhaps surprising exceptions in areas such as a school's extra-curricular programme, but thought needs to be given to how this can be extended if children are going to leave school with the important transferable skills needed for the future.

If you can design a programme with the flexibility to address the current issues of the day, then the curriculum can be made more relevant. Developing an understanding of climate change is just one example, borrowing from science, mathematics, the humanities and technology. After all, few rewarding careers expect workers to think in silos and subjects. As another example, all too often debating clubs are seen as bolt-ons, but presentation and argument are central to many areas of work. Shouldn't schools be looking to put debate at the forefront of the curriculum? Teachers and pupils often recognise the need for this but unfortunately schools operate in a high-stakes system where student voice is all too easily lost and schools are tied into superficial accountability regimes that produce too many losers – that's pupils as well as schools themselves. It shouldn't come as a surprise that company CEOs regularly berate school leavers for a lack of basic decision-making skills, little common sense and seemingly being incapable of holding a formal conversation. Rather than knowledge for its own sake, tested through an individual examination that may have little relevance to the real world, we need a curriculum where students can develop their understanding of the importance of competencies in areas such as teamwork. But we have recently moved in the opposite direction at secondary level. Project and coursework have largely disappeared at GCSE. Even investigative work in science has been squeezed out to the point where you can get a qualification in science without taking part in scientific experimentation.

The generic skills that students will need for a successful future are generally no longer disputed, but schools struggle to embed these and mapping them across the curriculum presents an almost impossible challenge. Not having to follow the National Curriculum should be a huge advantage for independent schools, giving them more control. Even the Independent Schools Standards Regulations that are used to frame the curriculum are encouraging. Rather than specific subjects, children in private schools should have a number of 'experiences', such as linguistic, mathematical and scientific, which can be delivered according to the best needs of the pupils. Despite that, most independent schools miss the advantages of such freedoms, preferring to divide the curriculum into an industrial model that has more to do with convenience than need, and still pays unquestioning homage to the false gods of terminal examinations and league tables, even when recognising that this may not be in the best long-term interests of the students themselves. Even when children are taken off timetable for the day, perhaps through a whole-school offsite experience, giving them a rare real-world experience, many teachers wedded to their subject silos will raise a note of protest. Few are brave enough to challenge a legacy mindset where the pervading expectation is of children who must fit in with the school, and it's a child's fault if she or he fails. Learning is more powerful and relevant when it's a shared, social experience. But education in many schools is now so compartmentalised that children and often teachers see learning as an hour's slot on a timetable. With content seeming so divorced from reality, children are left making subject and potential career choices on the basis of superficial measures, such as their experiences of a teacher or choices made across peer friendship groups. High university undergraduate drop-out rates are just one eventual consequence, as are misguided and inappropriate career choices for too many young people.

What are your thoughts on technology in schools?

We have to recognise that some of the technological developments creeping into pedagogy aim to address teaching expertise shortages. A growing number of teachers are being asked to teach in subjects beyond their qualifications and experience. Further, many schools investing in teaching systems find themselves in a spiral of rising costs, when abandoning a particular technology strategy can seem too daunting. New tech that promises the earth is sometimes difficult to evaluate and even more difficult to resist as part of a comparative arms race across schools. Many of the AI-related products marketed to schools have anything to do with AI, but they can look impressive in a prospectus. Technology has its place of course, and is at its best when enhancing the teaching and learning experience – but rarely in isolation from a teacher. And technology doesn't have to comprise of the latest technological bells and whistles. Video production and presentation has been widely used in schools, encouraging children towards teamwork, information selection, and drafting and scripting, among other transferable skills. Children enjoy the variety of social and emotional experiences that might be involved, further encouraging effective learning. It's not just technology for its own sake.

Atlas of the Future case study: Growing a world wonder

Great Green Wall

Africa is building a great big wall of trees through 11 countries, just under the southern edge of the Sahara Desert. Spanning the entire width of Africa – nearly 8,000 kilometres from Dakar to Djibouti – the Great Green Wall is planned to defend land from winds and sand.

The band of trees is designed to halt the advance of the desert and create a panoply of initiatives – providing food, jobs and a future for the millions living on the frontline of climate change. Answering many of today's most critical issues, it's a growing response to challenges from food security to migration, international peace and security. The drought-resistant Acacia tree has roots that hold water and provides shade.

Temperatures in the Sahel and the Sahara regions are rising faster than anywhere else and its populations are some of the poorest in the world. Human pressure on fragile ecosystems, alongside the effects of climate change, has led to poor soil quality, lower crop production and less grazing for livestock. Many people, especially the young, have left to find jobs elsewhere through migration to Europe or South America.

During the COP21 Paris talks in December 2015, world leaders and heads of international agencies pledged US$4 billion over five years to step up the initiative. Over the next ten years the project aims to reclaim 50 million hectares of land and sequester 250 million tonnes of carbon. These resources and crop production will help to feed the millions of people that go hungry in the region each day.

The first initiatives began in 2008 with the collaboration of 20 countries, planning choices of vegetation, working with local populations and plantings and land restoration – especially in Ethiopia, Senegal, Nigeria and Sudan. Senegal alone has now planted over 11.4 million trees and restored over 25,000 hectares of degraded land. Search engine Ecosia reports having planted over three million trees, mostly in Burkina Faso, as part of the project.

The Great Green Wall has been described as a 'generation-defining' project and now a virtual reality film lets you explore life beside the wall, following a Senegalese girl and her family at www.youtube.com/watch?v=sKInZTWT1c8.

Discover more online: https://atlasofthefuture.org/project/great-green-wall/

Project 6: Take a stand (Key Stage 2)

Welcome to this five-lesson project which asks pupils to create their own letters and videos to be shared with the local community in response to the issue of climate change.

Lesson 1

This lesson is an opportunity to discuss climate change rationally, hopefully straighten out some of the children's thinking and make them feel more empowered to do something about it!

Introduction (10 mins)

Ask pupils what they already know about climate change. Make notes on the board of what they know and also what they don't know. Use this as a time to discuss hopes and fears around this often emotional topic.

Main (40 mins)

Part 1 (20 mins): Ask pupils if they know who Greta Thunberg is. Show some of the videos of her campaigning and the speeches that she is making; fridaysforfuture.org is a great website which has collected her speeches together.

Challenge pupils to record examples of powerful vocabulary, key phrases and emotive language on sticky notes or a large sheet of paper for a working wall. Discuss how Greta gets her message across to her audience.

Part 2 (20 mins): Hold a whole-class discussion on climate change. What could be done? How could the class bring about change? You may want to split the class into smaller groups to discuss and then compare their ideas. You can appoint note-takers and discussion leaders, or practise turn-taking through passing a token.

Use the questions below to focus on what should or should not be done. Remember that the focus of the project is letter-writing, so steer the discussion to the industry, politician or community that you'll be addressing.

- What is an appropriate response to climate change?
- Who has the power to make changes?

- How can we contact people who have more power?
- How can we respond from the classroom?

Plenary (10 mins)

Summarise key messages and create a short plan of action for the rest of the project with the pupils. The plan will be to raise awareness of climate change in their community by writing letters to people who they think can affect change (local MP, councils, large businesses) and to create an open letter video to share their message with everyone at school in assembly.

Your plan of action should include who the pupils will be contacting, what they want to say and what changes they want to bring about.

Teaching tip

Throughout the lesson, it is really helpful if all of the large sheets, shared vocabulary and any other materials created can form a working wall for the pupils to work from and absorb. This really impacts positively on their final work.

Lesson 2

In this lesson, pupils study a letter and its structure before beginning to write their own.

Introduction (5 mins)

Display the example letter 'Humberdill Farm School's letter' on page 85 (also available to download from the online resources) on the board and examine the letter structure. How is the letter laid out? Use the IWB or a large piece of chart paper ruled into three rows, labelled 'Introduce', 'Inform' and 'Instruct'. Use these to help pupils to understand the structure of the example letter paragraphs, and think about how effective each paragraph is.

For each of the three sections, identify and note down the vocabulary and grammar which has been used to introduce, inform and instruct. Using sticky notes, ask groups of pupils to note down further examples for each paragraph to add to the working wall.

Main (45 mins)

Planning the introduction (25 mins): Focus on the 'introduce' section of their letter – prompt pupils to think about the audience they are writing to and why it is important. Think about the letter as a whole and ask pupils to discuss the following questions in groups:

- What will make it an effective letter?
- What makes a letter powerful?
- What style will it be written in?
- What is the aim of the letter?

Review who they will write to, to 'inform and instruct' to stand up against climate change. For example, it could be parents, a local business, the local MP or the local council. Tell pupils their letters will really be sent to their chosen person to give them purpose. You could have each group writing to a different person, each pupil could make their own decision or you could pick one place to send them all. Having one place that everyone writes to makes for much easier filming of your video letter.

Model writing the opening paragraph to a letter – the 'introduce' paragraph. This should include present tense verbs and pronouns, and clearly inform the audience who the letter is from and why they are writing. For an added challenge, pupils can identify the past progressive in the example opening ('we have been') and compare it to the present tense.

Example

Dear _____,

   We are the children from Class 4J at Humderdill Farm School in Coventry. We have been researching the effects of oil exploration on climate change and we are shocked by what we have found. Our class has used research books, infographics and the internet to uncover the truth about climate change, and, consequently, we have a message for you.

Writing the introduction (20 mins): Ask pupils to work independently to write their own letter introduction, including pronouns and present tense verbs and making sure they are thinking about who they are writing to – the style should be appropriate for the audience. Use ideas gathered earlier in the lesson too.

Plenary (10 mins)

Ask pupils to read aloud their completed introductions to a partner. Then, tell them to identify pronouns, present tense (and past progressive) and look for areas of success and improvement in each other's introduction.

Humberdill Farm School's letter

Humberdill Farm School
Arpee Road
Coventry
CV1 1LT

Friday 23rd February 2020

X-T Plastics
Redhill Road
Coventry
CV7 0UC

Dear Sir/Madam,

We are the children from Class 4 at Humberdill Farm School. We have been researching the effects of oil exploration in order to create plastic on climate change, and we have a message for you. It is time to stop and take responsibility for the position of power you hold over the future of our planet.

Our world is the only one we have. You may see this as your world – one you can take from without giving back. The effects of oil exploration and the creation of more plastics means that excess carbon dioxide is being added into our atmosphere, endangering the delicate balance of gases that block our planet from the sun's harmful rays.

We understand that this is not a simple issue. However, we would like to see you making a commitment to finding more green energy solutions, and by using recycled plastics instead of making more. In this way, we can save our world for a cleaner and safer future. We are looking forward to your reply, and to understanding how you will help make this change.

Yours sincerely,

Class 4, Humberdill Farm School

Lesson 3

In this lesson, pupils use their research to write the 'inform' section of their letter.

Introduction (10 mins)

Give pupils a few minutes to talk in their groups about the information they have so far, then challenge them to remember the structure of a letter and the key features. Also go over modal verbs, rhetorical questions and repetition before the next section.

Watch Greta Thunberg's EU speech (www.youtube.com/watch?v=FWsM9-_zrKo). As they watch it, ask pupils to listen out for examples of modal verbs, a rhetorical question and repetition for effect. Quickly make a list of modal verbs on the working wall.

Main (40 mins)

Part 1 (20 mins): Ask pupils to independently write down two key facts that they think they need to inform their addressee: the person or company they are writing to. Share these facts, and use a working wall or any evidence from Lesson 1 to start building a clear picture of what people need to know.

As a class, decide on the most important messages for the 'inform' section of the letter. Remind children of the three features to include:

- a rhetorical question
- modal verbs
- repetition for effect.

Part 2 (20 mins): Tell pupils to use the working wall as a scaffold and write their own 'inform' section independently, using the sentence level aim and class plan.

> **Teaching tip**
>
> This would be a good opportunity to draw together a focus group. It might be for less-able writers to create a shared text, or to challenge more able writers as they write independently.

Plenary (10 mins)

Invite volunteers to read out their work at the front of the class as though they are delivering a speech. Discuss the following questions as a whole class:

- How should their performance look?
- What makes a good performance?

This is a good moment to video pupils, watch them back and talk about their performance.

Teaching tip

Again, throughout the lesson, it is really helpful if all of the large sheets, shared vocabulary and any other materials collected can form a working wall for the children to work from and absorb. This really impacts on their final work.

Lesson 4

In this lesson, pupils write the 'instruct' section of their letter, deciding what action they want the addressee to take.

Introduction (5 mins)

Ask pupils to work in pairs. They should explain to each other why they are writing a letter – what response do they want? What are their aims? What do they want the person or company to actually do to prevent or help against the impact of climate change? Make notes on the board or working wall.

Main (50 mins)

Part 1 (35 mins): Model the subjunctive form and explain that this suits our formal letter (the subjunctive form shows both urgency and importance and expresses hopes for the future).

Example

If you were to reconsider your use of plastic straws, there would be less pointless plastic pollution in our local environment.

On mini-whiteboards, tell pupils to prepare one subjunctive sentence for use in their writing later in the lesson. Get them to then peer-improve their subjunctive form sentences with a partner, share some aloud and retain them for later.

Explain that today, pupils are going to write the instruct section of their letter – what do they want the addressee to do? How can the addressee make a change? Ask them to share ideas in their group and then feedback as a whole class. You may want to make a final decision on the one thing they want the addressee to actually do as a class to put in your video.

Then, tell pupils to work individually to write their final section. You may wish to draw together the same focus group as in Lesson 3. Ensure that children include their subjunctive form in their paragraph. Remember to tell pupils not to sign off their letters yet!

Draw the class back together and model a final sentence which shows that they expect a reply. For example, 'In anticipation of your response…' or 'I look forward to hearing that…'

Tell each pupil to write one final sentence: the expectation that the letter will be replied to.

Part 2 (15 mins): Now the letters are complete, pupils need to work on peer-editing so they are ready to be written up and sent. Get pupils to work with partners to read and make suggestions for each other's letters, before editing and improving. Share useful strategies for editing, such as using more appropriate or powerful vocabulary, varying sentence length for impact or using punctuation to communicate their message more effectively.

Plenary (10 mins)

Have a practical discussion about how to find the address for the people pupils are writing to. Use an internet search to find the addresses of local businesses, or for the office of the local council or MP. You could supervise a pupil as they ring a business and ask where correspondence should be mailed to. Have some envelopes ready for pupils to write addresses on or one large envelope for all the letters. Alternatively, this could be made simpler by writing an email, which could be shared and collaboratively written on the board before sending (although it must be said that an email is often ignored).

Lesson 5

In this lesson, pupils use their work so far to collaborate on an open letter and create a video to share in assembly and online.

Introduction (5 mins)

Watch the example videos of an open letter video:

- https://spark.adobe.com/video/96UsDdr0vxO2f
- www.youtube.com/watch?v=aP43b5LPQC8

A video letter puts more pressure on the person or company you're writing to to respond and make changes. Explain the value of collaboration to make the best possible version of their ideas.

Main (50 mins)

Part 1 (20 mins): Ask pupils to work in pairs to highlight or underline their best sentence from each section (introduce, inform, instruct) and together using their ideas, write a class version ready to be recorded.

Part 2 (30 mins): Film or record the voice of each pupil reading a sentence of the letter. Ask the pupils to speak loudly and confidently: they must be convincing in their delivery! For any parts that have a voice-over, use the Adobe Spark Video free image library to find an appropriate image or get pupils to act out an appropriate scene on camera instead.

Those who are less confident at delivery could do the filming rather than performing.

Plenary (5 mins)

Now you have recorded the letter, discuss with the pupils how and when they will show their video in assembly. Who should they invite? Who can they share it with to make sure their message is heard? The local press? Other companies or people associated with those you're writing to?

Chapter 7
Mental mastery

Introduction

The issue of children's mental health has become an area of real concern across the UK in recent years. Campaigners and research bodies are shining an increasingly critical spotlight on the ways that children are being manifestly let down by a broken system, with dozens of reports being published yearly highlighting the scale of the issue.

In this chapter...

In this chapter we will look at the scope of the mental health crisis in the UK, unpack just how we got here and consider where the responsibilities lie in providing support and education. An insightful interview with positive mental health writer, Natasha Devon, provides some practical advice that can be used to broach the topic of mental health with children. We also delve into the world of men's mental health and how a quarterly magazine called *CALMzine* provided a platform to normalise conversations about the all-important issues men face. In the five-lesson Mental Mastery project, your pupils will learn about mindfulness and meditation as essential tools for positive mental health, before creating their own walk-through video meditations.

The scope of children's mental health in the UK

Mental health problems come in many complex forms, affecting both adults and children at staggering rates within the UK.

According to a recent report by the NHS, one in every eight children in the UK is thought to have some form of a mental disorder. This means that four children in every class of 30 could be dealing with challenging emotional disorders, from depression and anxiety through to behavioural disorders. Not all of these children will be diagnosed, and of those who are, many are likely to be outside of any supportive care.

The reasons behind a growing mental health epidemic

Today's young people are growing up in unchartered territory. We are seeing the first generations of young people who've never known an analogue world, or a society not driven by austerity.

From a very early age, a child's world view and sense of reality is now enormously affected by the pressures of social media. They assimilate gender expectations, feel pressured to act as adults (and operate in an adult world) long before they have the emotional resilience to do so, and seek constant public approval for their appearance and character.

Alongside this, Bernadka Dubicka, the chair of the faculty for child adolescent psychiatry at the Royal College of Psychiatrists, cites education as also playing a key role: 'Education is a big contributing factor… the system assessment is causing stress and strain for young people, but within the context of us living in an uncertain world and them having an uncertain future… They worry about unemployment, student fees and those who are not going to college worry about how they are going to make a living and what the future holds for them.'

Though the mental health crisis affects children from all socio-economic demographics, children from single-parent families, or whose parents were unemployed or had no educational qualifications, are most likely to be affected.

UK children are falling through the gap

Despite the scale of the issue, the children's commissioner for England, Anne Longfield, published a recent analysis of the situation, in which she cited that only a 'small fraction' of children affected with mental health disorders were getting the support they needed.

As Anne Longfield writes in her analysis, 'There is still a vast gap between what is provided for children suffering from mental health problems and what is needed to treat them. The current rate of progress is still not good enough for the majority of children who require help.'

An 'intolerable' healthcare crisis

Teachers' leaders have said schools are at breaking point in dealing with the challenges of mental health issues in the classroom, saying they feel incapable of coping with the demands of student mental health needs.

As Louise Regan, the former president of the National Education Union, recently said, 'Teachers are overwhelmed by the sheer number of students showing signs of mental health problems… There is more focus on attainment measures rather than overall concern about the wellbeing of a child.'

As school funds have been progressively squeezed, key support roles within the education setting have been severely cut back. Many schools are simply unable to provide counsellors or pastoral care staff. The impacts of this are having a catastrophic effect.

As the mental health campaigner Natasha Devon put it, 'Most schools no longer have money for a personal, social, health and economic education teacher, leaving a gap in learning about mental health and body image.'

To plug this gap, the Department for Education recently issued a guidance document for schools, advising how to recognise the signs of mental health problems such as anxiety, depression, self-harm and eating disorders, as well as how to refer children to the local support services. But many teachers feel that this intervention falls woefully short of actually resolving the burden placed on schools to deal with a growing healthcare crisis.

Mental health in a criminal justice system

Without an adequate support structure within the school environment, and without access to mental health services, where do young people turn?

In England and in Wales, the police department has become a common helpline for mental health calls, as many people simply don't know who else to go to for help. According to a 2017 report, police in London receive a mental-health related call once every four minutes.

This often leads to the evidently troubling issue of people with complex mental health conditions being processed within the criminal justice system. In half of all mental health-related calls, distressed people find themselves being taken to a place of safety (which may sometimes be a police cell) by the police, rather than the ambulance service.

It is not the role of the police to patch up a broken mental health system, and despite their best efforts, the current situation is placing an intolerable burden on both the police and those most in need of help.

What is the government doing to tackle the mental health crisis?

In light of the catastrophic failures of the current system, David Cameron promised to give NHS child and adolescent mental health services in England £250 million more a year every year between 2015 and 2020.

Theresa May took this a step further, unveiling ambitious plans to expand NHS services for troubled youngsters and do much more to identify problems early by giving schools a key role in mental health support for young people.

Last year, this manifested as a £300 million mental health plan for schools. Some of the key tenets of the plan are to incentivise every school and college in England to have a senior responsible person for mental health, to establish support teams to liaise between schools and the NHS, and to trial a maximum four-week wait time for mental health services.

Despite the promising nature of the plan, the government only aims to put them in place in a fifth of the country by 2023, leaving large swathes of the UK's children dangerously under-serviced.

Children's charities, the National Audit Office and various education select committees have all said that the pledge is nowhere near adequate to meet the growing demands of the mental health problem in the UK. Even under the NHS's existing plans, the proportion of under-18s getting care when they need it will only rise from 25 per cent to 35 per cent by 2021.

A national responsibility

The figures paint a bleak picture: rising suicide rates, inadequate funding and a lack of cohesive direction about how to resolve the problem. The net result of this situation is that children are suffering.

When mental health issues are left untreated in childhood, they are likely to persist long into adulthood. Every young person who is unable to access the support they need risks becoming yet another future adult who is unable to function successfully within society, both on a personal and social level.

It's time to give children's mental health the attention it deserves and recognise it for what it is: a crisis of national responsibility.

Interview with Natasha Devon

Introducing...

Natasha Devon MBE is a writer and activist. She tours schools, colleges, universities and events throughout the world, delivering talks as well as conducting research on mental health, body image, gender and social equality. She campaigns both on and offline to make the world a fairer place. Natasha regularly speaks in Parliament and gives evidence to the Education and Health Select Committees, representing the interests of teenagers and teachers.

Whilst many of us are aware of mental health as an issue, can you explain how you interpret mental health in an everyday context?

One of the most important parts of my work is about making people realise that everyone has mental health but not everyone has a mental illness. We're taught a binary view of how someone might have had mental illness and then they recovered but it's much more of a process whereby our mental illness status can fluctuate. You can live with a mental illness and still be successful, just like a physical illness, by learning the adjustments you need to make to live alongside that illness.

I like to refer to a matrix with mental illness on one axis and mental fitness on the other. A mental illness can be something that we inherit or something that develops over time but mental fitness is always something that we can work on. If you have a child who has no symptoms of mental illness but no mental fitness tools to deal with challenges like bullying, death, divorce or moving schools, then they are only a few steps away from entering into the vulnerable part of the axis. Mental fitness is about strengthening that part of the axis so that, regardless of mental illness, they can be in a safe place. Young people need to understand that it's as important as eating your fruit and veg; it's your mental health five a day.

How does poor mental fitness develop?

The crucial thing to understand is that we have control over our mental fitness and we should be trying to nip things in the bud and empty the stress bucket daily if possible. However, there's an unhelpful culture in which too many pupils feel like they're not allowed to fail at anything. It's crucial that we recognise the point at which diminishing returns kick in when we stop doing the things that keep our mental fitness topped up. Many children are going into exam periods saying, 'I love the violin' or 'I love my sports club but I'm not going to do them now so I can focus on my exams.' These things are sometimes being seen as optional extras but they're not. Children need them more than ever because they help them to manage their stress levels. Long term, stress impairs their cognitive ability and will adversely affect exam results. Working too hard and perfectionism are two flaws that nobody minds admitting they have and this as a culture needs addressing.

How can we start the mental health conversation with young people?

What I always say to adults is that they should imagine it to be like opening a door and taking a step back. I often find that parents will only try to talk to their children about their emotions when it's already an issue which is too late. My approach with prep and primary pupils is to have a daily check-in about their feelings so that they can understand more easily what their normal baseline is. Once that becomes a routine, it becomes easier to identify over a longer period of time if they have deviated from that baseline.

With older students who feel emotionally overwhelmed, I give them three pieces of paper: 'problems I have no control over', 'problems I need someone's help with', 'problems I can solve myself'. Then I get them to destroy the one they have no control over because then they are left with a 'to do' list. As human beings, we tend to collect our worries, regardless of what they are and whether we can do anything about them so it's important to distinguish between them.

I also ask young people to think about their network. Often, they have a pastoral lead, a school nurse or that one teacher everyone loves who has queues of children at the door at lunchtime. But they can get equally good advice from a range of other people. Sometimes, they need tough love but some days you need someone to listen and ask open questions and tell you it's going to be okay. One of the best skills we can teach young people is to discern who they need to speak to on different days.

How can the curriculum support mental health?

The curriculum needs redesigning because we now know so much more about neurological development. We know that a teenage brain is very different from an adult brain and we know that a child brain is very different from a teenage brain. The very idea that we are suddenly an adult at 18 is ridiculous. Our brains don't finish developing until our mid-20s. Between the ages of nought and seven, we lay down all our fundamental psychological programming, absorbing the world like a sponge. Crucially, our brain develops back to front so reasoning doesn't really develop until seven. So, before that age, they're not thinking critically but rather learning through repetition. If a child is constantly being criticised or being given a line of thoughts about who they are and what they are about, they will swallow it whole and behave accordingly. We should therefore adapt our practice in schools to build a strong, emotional framework. Also, their daily habits are being formed which makes it a perfect time to introduce small routines like daily meditation and everyday discussions around mental health.

In terms of subjects, we all know how tough it can be to squeeze things into the curriculum, which leads me to believe that English as a subject can play a huge role. Creative writing can empty the stress bucket, get you into the moment and be very cathartic. Equally, a non-fiction project around mental health is a great way for children to learn about mental health in a non-judgemental way. Literature is also an excellent medium: Shakespeare in particular is a rich hunting ground. We have always been taught that *Romeo and Juliet* is a love story but it's about two young people who take their lives and four other lives in the process! Romeo is also probably bipolar. Similarly, Hamlet is very sleep-deprived and experiencing psychosis. These things can fuel a healthy classroom discussion about really important things that children might be going through, normalising things that are too often seen as taboo.

Atlas of the Future case study: Keep calm and save the male

CALMzine

A UK publication is on a mission to convey that it's OK for men to talk about sensitive things and mental health – because it's not cancer, road accidents, guns or knives that are the biggest single killer of men aged under 45 in the UK. It's suicide.

'We will all go through tough times in our lives, but men especially feel the need to pretend that everything is OK, and that admitting this to their friends will make them appear weak. I can assure you this is actually a sign of strength.' – Prince Harry.

Men tend not to talk about their issues in the same way as women do. Free quarterly men's magazine *CALMzine* aims to normalise conversations about the all-important issues guys face in the 21st century, breaking down the stigma attached to suicide. The charity behind it, CALM (Campaign Against Living Miserably), is dedicated to helping men ask for and receive support when down or in crisis. If men feel no shame in accessing help, the silence won't kill them.

The founder of CALM, Jane Powell, started the magazine to bust some of the myths around modern masculinity in 2009, launching it in TOPMAN in 2010. Editor Jojo Furnival wants to stress that it's not a 'mental health magazine'. Written 'by guys for guys', it is created by volunteer writers, photographers, artists and illustrators.

Mass media has a vitally important role to play in creating and heightening expectations. *CALMzine* offers an antidote to the offerings of 1990s 'lad mag' culture, which perpetuated unhelpful notions of masculinity – to men as well as women – from which some brands today are taking great pains to distance themselves: 'As an Editor, it's so refreshing to work on a publication that doesn't aim to put a rosy, glossy filter over everything,' Jojo Furnival notes. 'Real life isn't like that, and it can be a very lonely existence to believe that everyone else's life is picture perfect when yours isn't.'

Furnival commissions candid pieces about issues that face men today – from anorexia, anxiety and self-harm to health problems and life crises – alongside sport, music and men's interest articles. It's 'literary MANspiration'.

Ultimately CALM's mission is suicide prevention through solidarity, humour and community. Many readers become writers, volunteers or fundraisers, spreading the word as ambassadors. 'It's about creating a movement. The more we can say to guys, "It's OK that you feel like that; here's another guy who feels like that too", the more we can empower men (and women) to disassociate being "strong and silent" with masculinity.'

Discover more online: https://atlasofthefuture.org/project/calmzine

Project 7: Breathe (Key Stage 2)

In this project, pupils will write and record their own meditation video as well as have the opportunity to practise mindfulness and meditation themselves!

Teaching tip

Before the lesson each day, guide your class through a short meditation. Daily meditation scripts can be found online or videos can be found on YouTube. We recommend Headspace as a good place to start.

Lesson 1

Welcome to the first lesson in this mindfulness project. In this lesson, pupils are given an overview of the project and do some research on what mindfulness is.

Introduction (15 mins)

In groups, provide pupils with appropriate pages from the 'Mindfulness Explanation and Instruction Text' available to download from the online resources. Tell them to work together to identify the features of an explanation text.

Get pupils to share their ideas as a whole class and create a 'tick list' of features to include on a working wall. Guide them towards the following:

- Opening sentences giving a broad overview of what mindfulness is and why we should practise it.
- Captions to go with images, telling the viewer about the benefits of mindfulness.
- Rhetorical questions which draw the viewer in and can be used as part of an introduction.

- A 'Did you know' question and answer about mindfulness.
- Examples of temporal and causal conjunctions in sentences about mindfulness.
- Examples of formal voice in sentences about mindfulness.
- A glossary of terms about mindfulness.

Main (25 mins)

Get pupils to research 'What is mindfulness?' using the 'Mindfulness Explanation and Instruction Text' available to download from the online resources, books or internet searches. You may want to assign tasks to pupils based on ability.

Teaching tip

As the pupils are working, begin selecting ideas to use in the introduction to your video. These can also include stills and short videos showing the impact of mindfulness (relaxed, calm children!)

Plenary (20 mins)

Using the selected ideas, record some initial stills and short videos including the pupils' thoughts and ideas so far, as an introduction to a meditation video. Voice-over can be used over the still photographs of pupils (and some of the images provided) as well as pupils being videoed performing their sections.

Lesson 2

In this lesson, pupils have a chance to put Lesson 1's learning about explanation texts into practice. Based on your knowledge of your class, identify which word or sentence level features to focus on in this lesson.

Teaching tip

Before the lesson, guide your class through a second short meditation.

Introduction (10 mins)

Refer to the 'tick list' of features for an explanation text on your working wall from Lesson 1, and revisit the 'Mindfulness Explanation and Instruction Text' available to download from the online resources to remind children of the features needed for this genre of writing.

Having chosen the teaching points for your class, use the IWB slides to consolidate learning from Lesson 1. Use mini-whiteboards for pupils to practise writing sentences based on the sentence level or word level work chosen.

Example

All the pupils write a rhetorical question suitable for opening the introduction to the explanation text. They then write a sentence about mindfulness which uses a temporal conjunction.

All the pupils write a sentence about the benefits of mindfulness using formal language.

Main (40 mins)

Tell pupils to write their explanation text about mindfulness. Encourage them to use ideas from their research, the working wall and the 'Mindfulness Explanation and Instruction Text' available to download from the online resources.

Teaching tip

You may wish to draw together a focus group including pupils who need additional challenge or teaching, or work with a group to produce a shared write where everyone's ideas are discussed and written up into one group example by the teacher who models best practice.

Plenary (10 mins)

Using your school's editing process, ask pupils to select ONE section of their writing they would like to edit with a partner. Choosing one section enables them to focus and facilitates higher-quality editing.

Teaching tip

You may wish to set up stations around your room so that if, for example, they wish to edit their rhetorical questions, they go to the 'rhetorical question' table.

Lesson 3

In this lesson, pupils look at the features of instruction texts and plan their own writing. You may want to use some of the later pages in the 'Mindfulness Explanation and Instruction Text' available to download from the online resources, which are focused on activity instructions.

Teaching tip

Before the lesson, guide your class through a third short meditation.

Introduction (15 mins)

Discuss the challenge of writing your own meditation and brainstorm ideas for a 'tick list' of features to include. Write the ideas on a large sheet of paper for the working wall.

Identify prepositions and adverbials in the 'Mindfulness Explanation and Instruction Text':

- prepositions: while, after, during that minute, before you begin
- adverbial: before the sun went down, as fast as it could
- adverbs: slowly, carefully.

Elicit more examples from the pupils to build a vocabulary bank on a working wall.

Main (30 mins)

Spend some time looking at prepositions and adverbials. Use the words from the text as sentence starters for pupils to finish on mini-whiteboards.

Teaching tip

As an extra challenge for more able children, ask if they can use the prepositions and adverbials *within* sentences rather than just at the start. Can they use them where a new paragraph would start, to link ideas across paragraphs?

Using the provided model text (or an adapted version including features, vocabulary and grammar identified as next steps for your class), model writing an instruction text, called 'How to meditate'. Use mini-whiteboards for pupils to share ideas for some sections, as a shared write. Use a 'writer's voice' to verbalise your thought process as you write and model editing and improving as you work. Draw attention to the use of prepositions and adverbials (see annotated version).

Plenary (15 mins)

Encourage pupils to begin to plan and draft out their own meditation instructions ready for writing in Lesson 4. Tell them to include which prepositions and adverbials they will use in their writing and also to have a go at writing some full sentences. Use talk partners for pupils to share their ideas with a peer. Partners should check the use of adverbials and prepositions.

Lesson 4

In this lesson, pupils use their plan from Lesson 3 to write their own instructions independently. Sections from individual pupils' writing will be chosen to be included in the final class video.

Teaching tip

Before the lesson, guide your class through a fourth short meditation.

Introduction (5 mins)

Reread the modelled writing from Lesson 3 with the children, and revisit the vocabulary for instructions on the working wall (adverbials and prepositions). Remind pupils of the 'tick list' of features they all drew up together, and their own plan, which should include some prewritten sentences which they can simply transfer to their writing today.

Main (40 mins)

Pupils write their instructions for 'How to meditate'. This could be organised in several ways:

- Pupils write independently, with a focus group drawn together to produce a shared piece of writing. Draw your focus group together based on formative assessment – a group who all need guidance on the same next step.

- All pupils write at the same pace. For each section of the instructions, recap the main teaching points and vocabulary and then pupils all write their own version of that section before you all move on together.

- Partner-writing, where pupils use their individual plans but either work collaboratively on one piece by pooling their ideas or they write alternate lines of the same piece of writing.

Whichever model you choose, use misconceptions or excellent examples to run mini-plenaries.

Plenary (15 mins)

Using your school's editing policy, get pupils to edit their own or a partner's work. Whilst editing, look for sentences and sections which can be used for the final video. Pupils could begin to practise reading these out loud, using their best calm and relaxing voices!

Lesson 5

In this final lesson of the project, pupils practise reading aloud with the correct intonation and expression, before the final video is filmed.

Teaching tip

Before the lesson, guide your class through a final short meditation. You will also need to have selected sections from individual pupils' writing to be used in the class video.

Introduction (10 mins)

Collect ideas from the class about what could be included in your final video of your meditation (for example, a selection of still shots of calm images, some stills of pupils relaxing and some voice-over).

Main (40 mins)

Group the pupils according to the list of tasks decided on in the starter. You need to have pupils recording sections of their writing as voice-over, alongside pupils researching or filming calming photos or videos. Once they have collected the different bits of media, encourage pupils to start putting it together as a final video using Adobe Spark Video.

The final class video might follow this structure:

- a title
- an explanation about what mindfulness is
- a short guided meditation
- a 'thanks for watching'.

Teaching tip

Keep it simple and clear and you can't go wrong!

Plenary (10 mins)

If possible, share a selection of media from today's filming. (This can be done using an IWB casting app from your tablet to your board, such as AirServer, Reflector or via an adaptor). Discuss how intonation and expression have been used well to match the genre.

Chapter 8
Waste not, want not

Introduction

There are so many repeated behaviours that take place in society without us giving a second thought to why we do them. Some are completely logical and others, given some thought, are pretty strange. Queuing and Halloween are two that spring to mind. However, there are some things that happen which actually have way more of a profound and negative effect on our world than we could ever imagine. Food waste is one of them. The term refers to food that somehow manages to end up in the bins at home or out the back of our favourite supermarkets and restaurants. In addition to food wasted, a great deal of food is 'lost' before it reaches the retail environment.

In this chapter...

In this chapter we will unpack the statistics behind the amount of food waste in the UK and why this is the case. We look into the differences between food waste and food loss and how these differ around the globe, and consider what needs to be done to minimise these concerns. Hayley Connick, Managing Director of Too Good To Go, the world's largest marketplace for surplus food, shares her perspectives on the issues of food waste and what schools can do to help. Our Atlas of the Future case study examines Toast Ale, a beer brewed from leftover bread to fight food waste.

Why not continue focusing on the food waste issue, or perhaps choose plastic pollution, animal welfare or something of personal concern as a focus for the video campaign that the pupils will complete as part of the five-lesson Breaking Behaviour project? This persuasive writing project uses the creation of a video as a hook to encourage pupils to write about issues that concern them. They learn how to use their writing to start a campaign for positive change.

How much food do we waste?

A study was published in 2015 on food loss, which is the term given to food that does not complete the journey from field to supermarket shelf, focusing on the case of potatoes in Switzerland.

It found that over half of all potatoes were lost at some point in the supply chain, whether it be at the farm or at one of the various distribution centres along the way. Perhaps surprisingly, the most common reason for food being lost before it hits shelves was a cosmetic one. Some potatoes were simply deemed too ugly to be eaten (Willersinn et al., 2015).

Why is food waste a problem?

The amount of food being unnecessarily wasted is vast and, whilst there are various charitable organisations that work to redistribute some of the food that is lost from supply chains in the UK, hundreds of thousands of tonnes of perfectly edible food are still lost every year. When considered against the current backdrop of austerity, rising food prices and an increasing number of families dealing with food insecurity on a regular basis, having that many food items never make it to shelves is senseless.

Due to resource and funding restrictions, charities are not able to recycle more than ten per cent of food lost from UK supply chains (*Guardian*, March 2018). Much of the remaining 90 per cent could be going to feed the groups who are suffering the most – families with three or more children, and the unemployed, many of whom are increasingly reliant on food aid in the UK.

This is just one half of the problem. The other half lies in the volume of food being wasted after it has been purchased in shops.

There are charities and groups working to resolve this too, with some success. The amount of food wasted in the UK fell steadily between 2007 and 2014 but progress has slowed dramatically since then (*Guardian*, January 2017). The rate of change is slow, though, and it could be decades before 'avoidable' food waste accounts for less than half of total food waste.

The implications of food waste for UK households

Food insecurity is defined as a group or an individual going hungry, being at risk of going hungry, or being worried about going hungry because of a shortage of money.

Households that fall into the groups that are statistically most vulnerable to food insecurity (families with three or more children and unemployed people) are, however, already going hungry. In fact, figures released in 2018 estimated that one in every three households at risk of food insecurity was skipping meals in order to get by, and more than one in every ten larger families had taken food parcels at some point over the previous 12 months (*Guardian*, January 2018).

These groups are rapidly running out of support options. Food banks up and down the UK are already oversubscribed, and cuts to benefits continue to bite the lowest income groups. The full extent of the impact that the introduction of Universal Credit in the 2010s will have remains to be seen, but the likelihood is that low-income households will become more reliant on external support to feed themselves and their families.

Food waste and the growing population

The population of the UK is at its largest ever, topping 66 million people last year and growing (on a global scale) year on year.

One of the biggest challenges that we face as a planet is feeding this growing number of people. Food waste and food loss have a huge environmental and human impact, which will only get worse as global populations increase. This impact can be significantly lessened by reducing waste up and down global food supply chains. The implications of not taking any action, given the current rate of population growth, are dire.

Western diets in particular consist of high levels of meat, which is one of the most resource-intensive food products, using far more space and water than wheat, maize, rice, fruits and vegetables. If the population in developed countries continues to increase, demand will soon outstrip the available resources. This could have various financial and ecological knock-on effects. Increased demand and reduced supply will invariably push prices up, forcing more families into food insecurity, and the environmental impact could be catastrophic.

A great deal of work is being done to find ways to feed the global population, including increasing the productivity of land used for farming, reducing the amount of resource competition from other markets and working towards more stable fertility rates in developing countries.

There is substantially less of a focus on the problems of food waste and food loss at a domestic level, though. This could be because the problems are less visible and harder to understand. The nature of the challenge is different in different parts of the world as well, which creates even more complexity in finding possible solutions.

> **Talking point**
>
> What happens to the food that isn't eaten in your home? Does it get recycled or do you throw it away? What could you do to help food-deprived people in your area?

What can schools do?

How can we help our pupils relate to these global issues? We need to start small and close to home. Why not create a food waste committee who encourage the school to collect their food waste, be it from a school-provided lunch or packed lunches from home. Place food bins in classrooms or in the playground to capture wasted snacks. Collate the waste weekly, weigh it and create a bar chart in a visible place to highlight the results to the school community. The waste food committee can deliver assemblies about the concerns, share the school's data and challenge their fellow pupils to reduce the weekly statistics by being more selective in what they want to eat and how much they need to feel satiated. This can then be extended by pupils replicating this in their own homes and with their wider family and friends. Who knows where this might take them next?

Interview with Hayley Connick

Introducing...

Hayley Connick is a start-up/scale-up veteran with a big passion for food and a deep concern for the future of our little planet. She was able to combine all three when she was asked to lead Too Good To Go in the UK - the world's largest B2C marketplace for surplus food.

What's the single biggest challenge in tackling food waste?

Blue Planet opened our eyes to the dangers of single-use plastic and its impact on the planet. While the damage caused by plastic is now better understood, many people don't realise the harm that food waste causes the environment. Food waste is a major cause of CO_2 and methane emissions. If food waste were a country, it would be the third largest emitter of greenhouse gases, after China and the US. In fact, wasting food contributes around eight per cent of total human-caused emissions. Given that 70 per cent of food waste in the UK happens at home, it is imperative to raise awareness and educate people on the environmental consequences of wasting food in order to motivate them to change their habits.

This is no small task. We've become very cavalier about food. Post-war generations whose parents experienced rationing had much more respect for food – it was regarded as a precious resource, never to be squandered. Over the last few decades, food has simultaneously become cheaper and more ubiquitous and we've lost our connection to it. We no longer understand where our food comes from or the resources that go into producing it, which, in turn, means it's devalued and perceived as easily disposable.

It's not surprising therefore that we buy too much and don't think twice about throwing it away. According to Wrap, the average British family throws away £60 worth of food per month. We need to both re-establish our respect for food and understand the consequences of discarding it.

If you could do just one thing to turn the situation around, what would you do?

We need a *Blue Planet* moment for food waste. This would generate public awareness, which could give birth to a movement that inspires and empowers everyone to take action. In turn, this would apply pressure on corporations, governments, manufacturers and other key players in the supply chain. Food waste would then be prioritised on the political and legislative agenda, for example, putting an end to confusing date labelling and encouraging businesses to redistribute their surplus food.

What is the business opportunity, if only from a community or PR perspective?

As consumers, we are becoming more and more aware of how our choices impact the environment. A 2015 poll by Nielsen of 30,000 consumers in 60 countries around the world revealed that 66 per cent of consumers are willing to pay more for sustainable, ethically produced goods. This is particularly true of millennials, 73 per cent of whom stated they would pay extra for sustainable choices.

Although younger generations claim to be making ever more eco-conscious choices in their spending habits, those aged 18–34 generate more avoidable food waste than any other age group, nearly 50 per cent more than those aged 65 and over.

Food businesses should see this as an opportunity to look for more ways to make themselves more sustainable and, in turn, more appealing to consumers who want to make 'green' choices when spending. For example, at Too Good To Go we work with businesses with surplus food to resell their unsold items to local consumers, reducing food waste, acquiring new customers and recovering sunk costs all in one hit.

How can we avoid a sense of overwhelm or defeatism with regards to food waste?

We often forget the power we have as individuals. The truth is, every little helps. Every action, every decision and every meal rescued from going to waste matters. It might seem that businesses are the main culprits when it comes to generating food waste, but actually most of it (70 per cent) happens at home. According to Wrap, UK households throw away an estimated 7.1 million tonnes of food every year – and five million tonnes of that is perfectly edible.

Instead of feeling like we are powerless to tackle the issue, we can take some easy steps to fight food waste in the home. Making a shopping list and sticking to it is a great first step. Storing food in the right place and at the right temperature makes it fresh for longer. Understand date labelling; for example, 'Best Before' dates are a guide and food is still safe after that date. Take simple steps like not peeling potatoes, or eating the broccoli stump, freezing leftovers, cooking meals from whatever is left in your fridge rather than ordering a take-away – the possibilities are endless!

What role can schools play?

Schools play a major part in shaping a young person's relationship with food. By stressing how food and our environment are connected, schools and educators can inspire the next generation to respect our planet and its resources, and teach children the real value of food.

A simple way to encourage children to respect food would be to demonstrate the life cycle of food production in a tangible way. Growing vegetables or window-boxes of herbs in the classroom would help to bring to life how long it takes food to grow and the amount of work and resource that goes into it.

If we're to meet the UN's Sustainable Development Goal to reduce per capita food waste by 50 per cent by 2030, engaging the younger generation is critical. We all have a responsibility to take action for our own behaviour and to educate and instil a reverence for food in others. And to eat the potato peel.

Atlas of the Future case study: Beer brewed from bread fights food waste

Toast Ale

Toast Ale is the UK's first beer produced with bread. The award-winning craft beer uses surplus fresh bread from bakeries and sandwich makers, raising awareness of food waste and giving all profits to the charity Feedback, who campaign to end waste at a systemic level. Their recipe replaces one-third of malted barley with fresh bread that would otherwise be wasted. And it tastes mighty good.

'Our award-winning range of craft beer uses fresh, surplus bakery bread that would otherwise go to waste and we pour all profits into charities creating a better food system.'

The process is otherwise the same as traditional brewing. A certified B-Corp, Toast have shared a recipe online so that homebrewers can experiment with their bread leftovers.

The first beer style was a popular Pale Ale. They successfully crowdfunded in March 2017 to brew two new beer styles – a Session IPA and Craft Lager. The new beer styles are now available to buy online and at a growing number of stockists.

Drinkers have been enjoying the beers so much since they launched in 2016 that they cracked a pretty amazing milestone – they have now brewed with over one million slices of surplus bread. That's a lot of beer, having a pretty awesome impact on the planet. They have got a big ambition: to rescue one billion slices of surplus bread.

Now they are launching a core range of craft beers in 330 ml cans. Why cans? 'Put simply, we love them. They're becoming more and more popular, with 25 per cent of UK craft beer sales in cans in 2018. They keep the beer tasting great and offer environmental benefits as they're lighter and easier to transport.'

It's a winning combination, proving that great-tasting craft beer can fight food waste for a better planet. In July 2019 Toast successfully raised £39,110 with 269 supporters in 29 days.

Discover more online: https://atlasofthefuture.org/project/toast-ale

Project 8: Change it

Change It is a persuasive writing project. Using video as a hook, this project educates pupils about issues which concern them and how they can make a difference by using their writing to spread the word about a campaign.

Lesson 1

This lesson is to help pupils understand how one person can bring about change in something they care about.

Introduction (15 mins)

Explain to the pupils that they are going to be planning and writing a campaign to bring about change for an issue they feel strongly about. They can choose any topic they like but it is highly recommended that you choose one issue as a class. As an example, introduce the campaign 'Stop The Rot': www.thisisrubbish.org.uk/stoptherot and show pupils their campaign video on Vimeo: https://vimeo.com/143823581

Watch the video and ask pupils to summarise verbally what they think the campaign was about in one sentence to a talk partner.

Main (30 mins)

Provide small groups with infographics and articles on your chosen topic. Pinterest is brilliant for infographics. Here are some links for food waste.

- High cost of food waste: www.globallandscapesforum.org/infographic/infographic-high-cost-of-food-waste
- Pinterest infographics: https://bit.ly/3daJfgk
- UN infographics: www.fao.org/save-food/resources/keyfindings/infographics/fruit/en/

Ask pupils, can they identify any particularly powerful sentences or phrases? Why are they powerful? Identify where words have been used very precisely to convey specific meaning. Identify examples of emotive language, persuasive language, rhetorical questions and short sentences. Begin a vocabulary working wall of powerful language to use in successful campaigns.

Plenary (15 mins)

Tell pupils to write a short tweet (around 140 characters or 30 words) or two to summarise their campaign's main issues. Encourage them to use some of the language gathered for the vocabulary working wall. Drafting their tweet on a mini-whiteboard first will help pupils to change vocabulary for maximum effect within the word count. Invite pupils to read out their tweets to the rest of the class and take feedback.

Lesson 2

This lesson is for pupils to understand the value of a persuasive letter for a successful campaign.

Introduction (5 mins)

Explain to the pupils that today they need to be really persuasive because they are going to be using a letter to contact someone of influence who can help with your campaign. In the case of food waste, this could be:

- your local supermarket manager
- a local restaurant owner
- your own school catering team.

Main (45 mins)

Drama (5 mins): Split the class into pairs for a short hot-seating activity. In each pair, one pupil takes on the role of interviewer while the other takes on the role of the influencer. They role-play a conversation where the interviewer asks the influencer what she or he is trying to achieve, and why. Listen out for any strong role-plays which can be shared with the rest of the class.

Reviewing an example (20 mins): Show the example letter 'Greenhill Primary School's letter' on page 114 (also available on the online resources), which could have been written for a campaign on plastic pollution. Identify that it is using a three-paragraph structure:

- introduce
- inform
- instruct.

In pairs or small groups, ask pupils to find examples of:

- a rhetorical question
- a short sentence for impact
- emotive language
- repetition (the final paragraph repeats the word benefit).

Depending on the needs of your class, you might also want to include some additional grammar work by adapting the example letter.

Introduction writing (20 mins): Using the letter as a scaffold, get pupils to write their own letter introduction paragraph to their person of influence about their campaign. Encourage them to use some of the language features identified above.

Plenary (10 mins)

Peer-editing: Pupils assess the work of their partner, trying to identify language features and strong persuasive phrases. Invite pupils of all standards to share examples of impressive introductions from their partners.

Greenhill Primary School's letter

Greenhill Primary School
Beverley
Yorkshire
YO6 3NX

Tuesday 27th June 2017

Super Supermarket
Lee High Road
Beverley
YO4 2ZX

Dear Mr Brown,

We are Amy and Ella Meek, two sisters who feel passionately about environmental issues which are harming our planet. We are writing to you because we are very worried about the problems caused by plastic bottles. Many people are beginning to realise that this is a serious problem. Wouldn't you like to keep your customers happy and have a positive impact on our beautiful planet?

When plastic bottles are thrown away, they do not disappear. They will be on our planet forever. The plastic used in water bottles eventually breaks down into very small pieces. These tiny pieces, and other plastic items which have been thrown away, make their way into our oceans and into our food chain. Most bottles are only used once before they are thrown away. They are thrown into landfill centres where they are burned or just left in nature as rubbish. This has to stop. Is this the planet we want to pass on to future generations?

There is an alternative. Supermarkets like yours could give customers a choice, such as selling water in cartons, boxes or cans. If you do this, we will benefit as customers and the Earth will benefit from less plastic pollution. Also, you will benefit because your customers will be more loyal to you when they see that you are trying to make a difference. Please don't leave the world with a problem that can't be fixed. Make a change now.

Yours sincerely,

Amy and Ella Meek

Lesson 3

In this lesson, pupils choose their strongest facts in order to highlight the importance of their campaign.

Introduction (10 mins)

Revisit the infographics that you looked at in Lesson 1. Ask pupils to revise the facts that they chose to see whether they still think they are the strongest ones that will convince others to join their campaign. For the main section of this lesson, they will need to have around three facts that they will use to write the 'inform' paragraph of their campaign letter. Share them as a whole class so that any pupils who are struggling can borrow ideas from others.

Main (40 mins)

Revise sentence level work (20 mins): Revisit the sentence level work from Lesson 2 so that pupils can reflect on their work and improve it in this lesson. They are:

- a rhetorical question
- a short sentence for impact
- emotive language
- repetition.

Using the board, revise rhetorical questions and show pupils how to add them to facts in order to increase impact.

Example

Over one third of food produced is never eaten. Think about that. It is either lost during the harvest or thrown away after not being sold in a shop. If you were starving, wouldn't this break your heart?

Writing the inform paragraph (20 mins): Pupils write at least three interesting facts about their campaign. Each of their facts should include a sentence level focus from the list above. This can be adjusted according to the ability of the children. These might be used as 'tweets' which provide a summary of the campaign for you, the teacher, to use on social media to generate a wider buzz about the work you are doing in class.

Plenary (10 mins)

Invite pupils to share one of their fact bytes with the class. After each sentence, the class should identify which sentence level skills have been used. Use this time to develop their public speaking skills as practice for filming the final video.

Teaching tip

It's a good idea to video some of the performances at this stage in order to develop pupils' enthusiasm for writing, give them feedback on their performance and show the class how to manage a quick filming session.

Lesson 4

In this lesson, pupils need to decide what they are going to ask of the influencer they are writing to, and write the final part of the letter.

Introduction (10 mins)

Brainstorm ideas for the kinds of things that pupils could ask of their influencer. On the board, draw a line down the middle and write 'What' on one side and 'Why' on the other.

Example

What do you want your influencer to do?	**Why** do you want them to do it?
We want you to organise food deliveries at the end of the day to the local homeless shelter.	It will improve your reputation in the community and make people support you by buying from your shop.

As a class, come up with as many of these as you can.

Main (35 mins)

Using colons (10 mins): Discuss the use of colons. They are used here in compound sentences to separate two independent clauses (clauses which make sense by themselves and *could* stand alone). The first clause gives a fact or opinion and the second gives further details. The two clauses joined together by a colon should be closely related in subject matter.

Example

You have the power to make a huge difference to our food waste problem: please don't waste this opportunity to use your influence.

Using the ideas from the introduction, get pupils to work in pairs to create examples of sentences which can be joined together.

Writing an ask paragraph (25 mins): Get pupils to write an ask paragraph including colons to join independent yet related clauses. This is a good time to revisit some of the sentence work from previous lessons:

- a rhetorical question
- a short sentence for impact
- emotive language
- repetition.

Plenary (15 mins)

As a whole class, take one pupil's instruct paragraph and work on it together. Work on making it emotional so that the audience feels compelled to do what you are asking them. Using short sentences towards the end might be a good way to focus pupils' improvements. Allow five minutes at the end for pupils to improve their own work.

Lesson 5

In this lesson, pupils film their campaign video.

Introduction (15 mins)

Start the lesson by watching some effective campaign videos made by other schools: www.youtube.com/playlist?list=PL_odjZ7bN8F4CIPgn7k4aeYjm6tbyE nHG. It is worth investing time in this as it makes a big difference to the end result. Discuss what makes them effective, thinking about:

- language
- delivery
- steady filming
- good sound
- clear message
- interesting visuals.

Main (30 mins)

There are now two ways to film your work:

- As a whole class, get different groups up one by one to film a section of their work.
- In groups, give pupils ownership of creating their own video. This relies on having one filming device per group. To make it more manageable, it is advisable to model how to do each section of filming and then allow groups to film their own. A big space is often needed so that sound issues are minimised.

Divide the work from the previous lessons into sections so that you have distinct sections to film. This is only a guide so feel free to do it however suits you best.

- Introduction, paragraph 1, talking to camera. This can be repeated by a few different pupils: it adds to the impact and gravitas of the video.
- Inform, paragraph 2, voice-over with images to illustrate your points. You can usually have about five different facts using five pupils' work.
- Instruct, paragraph 3, talking to camera. This can feature work from at least three different pupils.
- Ending. Ask some pupils to write a suitable ending to your video, a simple ten-second closing.

Example

Please show that you care by taking the time to reply to our campaign. We've worked really hard on it and feel very passionately that we need leaders like you to act. Many thanks.

Once pupils know which section they are responsible for, give them time to choose their most impactful sentences and rehearse. Then, use the rest of the session to record. For pupils who don't want to be on camera, remember that they can fulfil roles like camera person or director who controls the shoot. Also, one person's writing can be delivered by more than one person.

Plenary (15 mins)

Share your finished video clips for the whole class. If you can edit using a screen at the front of the class with your pupils, this is a very powerful experience for them. It also gives you the chance to improve, re-record if necessary and also crowdsource ideas on how to edit everyone's work together.

Chapter 9
Reading rocks

Introduction

Visit any teachers' forum, Twitter feed or in-person gathering, and there is a clear sense that reading is important and that it is a source of great pleasure. Teachers love it and understand its power on so many levels. However, the same cannot be said for young people. According to Nielsen's 2018 report, 'Understanding the Children's Book Consumer', only 32 per cent of 0–13s are read to daily and 29 per cent of 0–13s read for pleasure daily. Why is this a problem?

In this chapter...

In this chapter we will discuss the importance of reading and what it brings to a child's learning experiences. An interview with renowned children's author Michael Rosen explores his hopes and desires for education and we hear about the ingenious Drinkable Book: an instruction manual for making water clean enough to drink whilst using its pages as filters. Then, kick start your own reading renaissance with Michael Rosen leading you and your class through the five-lesson Video Book Review project.

Why read?

Perhaps not top of everyone's list of why reading should be encouraged, but of great importance nonetheless, is the impact that reading has on academic attainment. The OECD's 'Reading For Change' report showed that 15-year-olds from low socio-economic backgrounds who were avid readers achieved more academically than students from medium to high socio-economic backgrounds who were not engaged in reading. The report suggested that encouraging reading may be one of the most effective ways to bring about social change.

Do you enjoy reading? How has reading helped you? What or who inspired you to read?

Reading helps you grow mentally, emotionally and psychologically. Every book provides you with something new, such as a new way of understanding human interactions, a new way of using language for description or a new way to find enjoyment in life. However, reading does much more than this too. It helps you improve your focus, concentration and memory. Think back to the last book you read and how much information you had to remember as you went along – character names and relationships, names of places, plots and subplots, the sequence of events and much more. Reading expands your knowledge base and helps you become more aware of your surroundings and the wider world, helping you make better choices and decisions in life. It helps you discover yourself by opening up new dimensions of thought that you align with, dismiss or question. By immersing yourself in a book, you get drawn into the experiences and emotions being portrayed, imagining your reactions and decisions in those situations. Reading is a powerful tool for growth and learning but, above all, reading gives you joy and pleasure!

The beauty of reading is that, as long as a young person has access to books at home, through school or at a library, then no amount of money can help a child develop academically through reading more than any other, regardless of family income.

But perhaps academic progress isn't your priority and you're much more concerned about a child's wellbeing? As noted elsewhere in this book, we are currently experiencing never-seen-before levels of poor mental health in our young people. Data from the National Literacy Trust's eighth Annual Literacy Survey of 49,047 children and young people aged eight to 18 in the UK highlighted some interesting statistics about the connection between wellbeing and reading.

- Children who are the most engaged with literacy are three times more likely to have higher levels of mental wellbeing than children who are the least engaged (39.4 per cent vs 11.8 per cent).
- Children who are the least engaged with literacy are twice as likely to have low levels of mental wellbeing than their peers who are the most engaged (37.4 per cent vs 15 per cent).
- Children with above expected reading skills are three times more likely to have high levels of mental wellbeing than their peers with below expected reading skills (40.3 per cent vs 13.1 per cent).
- As children transition from primary to secondary school, their levels of literacy, engagement and mental wellbeing both begin and continue to decline.

Keen readers will anecdotally understand the joy, empathy and relaxation that come from regular reading and the statistics above around academic attainment and wellbeing are very compelling. Nevertheless, despite the overwhelming evidence that reading truly matters, there is still the problem of less than a third of children reading regularly. Why is that?

Egmont's 'Love Of Reading' report found that there are three key factors that affect reading for pleasure:

- School: the curriculum makes reading a subject to learn, not something to do for fun.
- Screens: increased screen time means less time for reading and other activities.
- Parents: lack of awareness that they need to read to their children beyond the point at which the child can read independently.

The context of screens is most interesting for two reasons. Firstly, as a big advocate of how the right technology can enhance teaching and learning, there needs to be a clear distinction between useful screen time and wasted screen time. Clearly, watching cat videos is fairly useless (unless it helps to improve your mental health after a tough day), whilst watching a History Bomb to help you remember the key events of World War Two is much more useful.

Secondly, whilst reducing useless screen time should be a priority, there is a good reason why so many of us are Netflix subscribers and why three times as many kids want to be YouTubers than astronauts: video is an incredible medium as well as an incredibly powerful medium. It's time to harness the power of screen to get young people reading as much as possible.

Talking point

How much screen time do you have? What do you mostly access during screen time? Do you prefer to read stories on devices or in books?

Share with the class

Kenny Bartonshaw and Dan Jones from The St. Bart's Multi-Academy Trust in the UK are two teachers who have combined YouTube with a love of reading perfectly across their schools. Instead of fighting the kids' desire to be on camera, they decided to capitalise on it as much as possible. Having trained all the teachers and children in how to write and film book reviews, they now have their own YouTube channel dedicated to book review videos. Such is the enthusiasm for reading across their schools, not to mention the quality of the videos, the library service in their local city are now featuring all their videos via QR codes on bookshelves so that other local children can be inspired to read. If you can't beat 'em, join 'em!

Reading needs to be at the heart of school life with opportunities presented in every classroom, corridor and learning environment, even outside. There are many ways that this can be achieved, including well-stocked classroom shelves representing a range of reading materials such as fiction, non-fiction and magazines, having inspiring displays, dedicated library time and word-focused playground markings.

But it is important to find ways to motivate pupils to read too. Encourage a whole-school culture of DEAR (Drop Everything And Read) or ERIC (Everybody Reading In Class) where the entire school community is timetabled to read, including the teachers, who are great reading role models; read out loud to the class each day; set a reading challenge for school holidays such as 'Extreme Reading', encouraging your pupils to take photos from peculiar places to read; provide a cosy reading corner with cushions and beanbags; let pupils use e-readers or listen to audio books; but above all, provide the time for reading to be done, keep it fun and create a positive ethos around reading.

Interview with Michael Rosen

Introducing...

Michael Rosen is an English children's novelist, poet and the author of 140 books. He needs little introduction to teachers. He served as Children's Laureate from June 2007 to June 2009. He has been a TV presenter and political columnist. Recently, he has become something of a YouTube celebrity with his own channel. As someone who is so revered by teachers for his work as a writer, his work as a YouTuber makes him a very interesting interviewee given how disinclined schools are in general towards digital media compared to the sacred act of reading.

I've done my research and so I know that you are a writer but who is Michael Rosen?

A writer sounds about right and also I've edited books. If you put them all together it's over 200 books. I'm also a broadcaster and the BBC invites me in to do programmes usually about language or literature mostly for radio. I also used to do a bit of children's TV. I would do more if they asked me!

I listened to your keynote at the Children's Media Conference in 2018 and found it fascinating that you were talking to a broadcast audience about how your YouTube channel is in direct competition with them. Could you tell me a little bit about your YouTube life?

I suppose it started partly because I don't get much television work now but I still enjoy performing. It's a way that schools can enjoy my work without me being there. For me, it's the perfect way to bypass the gatekeepers in the television industry. Bit by bit, my son Joe and I figured YouTube out and now we have nearly 400,000 subscribers and are approaching 100 million views. I enjoy it because you get an artistic freedom, which of course is not without its own responsibilities.

What is the point of education?

I suppose there are three ways of looking at that question; what does it mean from the child's point of view; what does it mean from the teacher's point of view; and what does it mean from society's point of view?

When society answers that question, or rather all these incredibly global people in the Department for Education, it's about knowledge transmission and cultural transmission. We have this enormous body of knowledge and wisdom and we've collapsed all that into this thing called the National Curriculum and then it's our job to transmit that.

Also, there are things like being nice to each other which schools are supposed to pass on in their various forms. Most teachers would think that it's incredibly important we create decent and good places where we treat each other properly and as equal or modelling that behaviour but of course that is to some extent enforced obedience.

If you look at it from the point of view of the parents and children, then there's a huge demand that in some way or another through school you will learn to do things like how to be happy or how to acquire things that will enable you to go through life.

For me, there's also something very important that is hard to put your finger on. Everybody has a culture, everybody comes from somewhere. Does a school say to you that you are a valuable and valid human being, that things that you do in your life are interesting things, that you have at home and that your grandparents are really interesting? Or does school say no actually, could you leave all that at the door because all the interesting stuff is here in the 11 plus or whatever book that we're doing – this maths book, this geography textbook – or does it ever open the door and say, 'Hey, what's going on here?'

What's the first thing that you would like to see taught in schools?

We do a lot to talk about language in schools. Most of it is focused on writing and most of the writing is what you might call continuous formal prose. So, the children have to learn how to construct sentences, paragraphs and chunks of writing whether it's a story or essay or composition. There's a tremendous weight of importance on this and that's fine. But as human beings, we communicate with each other with something else that's terribly important called conversation. Now conversation is not some sort of accident, it's not some sort of thing that just sort of happens by mistake. Conversation structures are extraordinary: how we take turns, how we can construct a thought or an argument in a conversation, how we can listen to other people, how I can influence you and you can influence me. Oracy and public speaking are becoming much more popular in school which is great but actually it's not only a matter of standing up, being able to talk for ten minutes or half an hour and convince and influence people. It's also about how we can chat and progress things. It's more like the art of negotiation. It's cooperative talk, it's conversation.

What's the second thing you'd like to see taught in schools?

I think that one of the most important things going on in the world right now is migration. The moment you start looking at the history of humankind it becomes a thing of migration. You've told me you come from Liverpool. You've migrated from Liverpool to London and some of your family came over from Ireland. As we know, Ireland massively depopulated many times over due to terrible famine. The issue of migration is in the news virtually every day with what Trump is doing and so this is an important thing to think about, especially because we need to understand that everybody at some point has been involved in migration. Even if you ended up just moving next door, as a child you have actually migrated to a completely different world. It seems to me that it's a huge aspect of human existence but when you look at the curriculum, it comes up in geography and history a bit but it doesn't show that every single human being that lives in the British Isles must have migrated at some time. It gets us thinking about cultural education as a constructed nation-state. The idea that we all belong to this nation is a form of education that we've been given so it seems to me to be important to study that.

What is the third thing you wish they taught in schools?

I wish they studied the future. On first glance, it's a very broad subject – it could be the future of work, it could be science fiction, climate change, the possibility of nuclear war. It's a very wide, eclectic subject to do which could also touch on the history of the future. If you think about the notebooks of Leonardo da Vinci, he drew a flying machine regardless of whether it could or couldn't work. The point was he was saying wouldn't it be great and isn't it possible for human beings to get into a machine and fly? He was projecting into the future what was possible and he was right. With children, we can start with getting them to think about what they're going to do tomorrow before moving on to ten years' time, 20 or 30 years' time. There's plenty to study in the future, isn't there?

Atlas of the Future case study: Pages to purify

The Drinkable Book

An estimated 750 million people worldwide drink and cook with water from a contaminated source every day. Providing cheap, clean drinking water for many people in the developing world, The Drinkable Book is an instruction manual educating on how to clean drinking water, with pages that can be torn out and used as water filters.

Developed over eight years by PhD student Dr Theresa Dankovich and her team, and partnered with non-profit WATERisLIFE, which has active field offices in Kenya and Ghana, each 'book' has 26 tear-out pages of powerful filters. Each purifying paper lasts from two weeks to a month, costs US$0.20 to produce and comes inscribed with essential information on safe water use. One book can provide safe water for up to four years.

Easy to use and relatively cheap to produce, informative design belies its complex chemistry. Working like a 'scientific coffee filter', each piece is coated with silver nano-particles that kill more than 99.9 per cent of bad microbes; pages can reduce bacterial levels and dilute raw sewage to the levels found in US tap water. Now engaged in a substantial scaling up of output, the project is seeking further funding whilst looking for ways to develop. One plan includes a new Willy Wonka inspired 'blueberry' book, just for kids.

Discover more online: https://atlasofthefuture.org/project/the-drinkable-book

Project 9: Video book review

Lesson 1

In this lesson, pupils learn about the features of a good book review and write their introduction. Before the lesson, select a book that the class knows well or is currently reading for their collaborative review.

Introduction (10 mins)

Explain that in this project, pupils will be writing a book review ready to share as a vlog. Take ideas from the class about why people would create and share book reviews (for example, to share thoughts and opinions about books, to comment on characters, to encourage others to read or to recommend a favourite book). Then, in talk partners, get pupils to recommend a book they have read and enjoyed to their partner. As a whole class, discuss which recommendations were successful and why.

Main (40 mins)

Part 1 (15 mins): Watch some video book review examples: www.youtube.com/playlist?list=PL_odjZ7bN8F7eXHSM00lnY6ay7VD7B43Y

Ask pupils which book review video was the best and why. Discuss how useful the content was for potential readers of the book. What are the key features and sections that a book review needs to include? Give each group sticky notes and ask them to record one idea per sticky note, then order them appropriately. Tell the groups to briefly walk around the other tables, looking at the ordered key features and sections.

As a class, agree on the sections to be included in the book reviews and the order they should come in. I recommend the following:

- introduction
- synopsis
- highlights (favourite character, favourite part and opinion)
- rating
- summary or conclusion.

Part 2 (25 mins): Using the example below, discuss the model introduction text, taking note of the use of a colon.

Example

Hello and welcome to our book review from Grove Primary School. I'm Fred and my class, 4B, are the best class in school: we work hard and have lots of fun!

Today, I am going to review the beautifully illustrated book, *Where the Wild Things Are* by Maurice Sendak, because I have read the book many times and I want other people to enjoy it as much as I do.

Using the whiteboard, show how a colon can be used to join two sentences, where the second sentence expands upon the first. Split partners into As and Bs. On mini-whiteboards or scrap paper, children in A write a sentence telling the reader about a book character (for example, Harry Potter is an amazing wizard). They find a partner in group B who then writes a second sentence, expanding on the first. Both sentences are joined using a colon (for example, Harry Potter is an amazing wizard: he could produce a Patronus charm aged only 13). Read some of the examples aloud, using any errors to make the teaching points:

- the two sentences (clauses) need to be independent and make sense by themselves
- the second one must tell us more about the first.

Using the model introduction text as a scaffold, tell pupils to write their own introduction to the book review video, including a sentence using a colon. They need to include the key points:

- opening line
- name of child and class (and why their class is the best!)
- name of the book and the author
- why they have chosen to review the book.

Plenary (10 mins)

Ask pupils: How do we make sure that people don't switch off our class video? Invite ideas. Refer to the videos seen earlier and comment on the performance: pace, pitch, tone and intonation. Model reading out loud, then invite children to read out their examples, focusing on performance. If you can, video an introduction or two and watch them back on the board, commenting on performance.

Lesson 2

In this lesson, pupils learn how to summarise a book (without giving too much away!) and write a short synopsis. They include the use of different punctuation to demarcate parentheses within a sentence.

Introduction (5 mins)

Discuss why, in our video book review, the book needs to be summarised but we must not give away too much of the plot. Explain that this is a book synopsis – it gives the review audience enough information about the book to interest them without any spoilers! Use a 15-second timer and, in talk partners, ask pupils to summarise their favourite book in 15 seconds. You may need to give them a few goes!

Main (40 mins)

Using the board, show the following model synopsis.

Example

Where the Wild Things Are is a prize-winning picture book for children and the young-at-heart. Max – who is sent to bed without any dinner – embarks on a fantastical adventure when his bedroom suddenly transforms into another world. He is amazed: his adventure is beyond his wildest dreams!

As a whole class, unpick the grammar and sentence structures, including where parentheses (added bits of information) have been demarcated using dashes. Use the board to show that brackets and commas could also be used. The model synopsis is exactly 50 words long! Tell pupils that their task is to summarise their chosen book in no more than 50 words themselves – no spoilers! Can they include an added extra bit of information (parentheses), correctly punctuated with either brackets, commas or dashes?

Plenary (15 mins)

Using talk partners and your school editing policy, tell pupils to work together to improve each other's work. Tell them to check that there are no spoilers, but that enough of the story has been shared to hook the audience. They should also look for parentheses and improve any vocabulary. Also, make sure the synopses are no more than 50 words long! While partners are doing this, take one set of partners and record their synopsis either as a voice-over or as a video. Once the rest of the class has finished editing, invite them to feed back on the recording you made. Comment on performance and choice of language.

Lesson 3

In this lesson, pupils explore their favourite characters or plot lines and write an opinion piece. They revisit the skill of using a colon to separate two independent clauses and expanding upon their ideas. More able writers are also introduced to the parenthetical afterthought.

Introduction (10 mins)

Choose a book character that the pupils in your class will know well, and describe them using three words. Can they work out the character? For example, 'gigantic, kind, ears' might describe the BFG or 'scar, wizard, glasses' might describe Harry Potter. Using talk partners, get pupils to describe a favourite character from their book using only three words, for their partner to guess.

Now choose a plot line from a book that your class will know and describe it using only one sentence. Can they guess which book it is? For example, 'A boy is wrongly sent to a prison camp for teenage boys and made to dig large holes in the desert' describes *Holes*. 'A boy with OCD who refuses to go to school and watches the world from his bedroom window helps to solve a crime' describes *Goldfish Boy*.

Again, get pupils to work in their talk partners to describe a book to their partner using only one sentence.

Main (40 mins)

Show the modelled character description below for the 'highlights' section.

Example

The main character, Max, is really fun to read about because he is naughty. I particularly like how he speaks to the Wild Things and how he sends them all to bed without any supper – just as his mum had done to him. I think that Max would be great fun to play with: his vivid imagination would mean that we were never bored. If you like getting up to mischief, then you will love Max, too!

Discuss the use of a colon (as in Lesson 1) and, for more able writers, discuss the use of the parenthesis at the end of the second sentence. (This is a parenthesis at the end of a sentence, demarcated with a single dash – a parenthetical afterthought.) If you want to challenge your class to use a parenthetical afterthought, use mini-whiteboards and start them off with a sentence to add a thought to. Choose a few to share with the class.

Get pupils to write a paragraph about a favourite character, using the modelled text as a scaffold. More able writers can also write a paragraph about their favourite plot line, giving their opinion on why it was their favourite.

Plenary (10 mins)

Share good examples of pupils' work. This is a good time to record a small selection of their work to be included in the video. For example, video one pupil as they read their favourite highlight (off camera) whilst other pupils act out the scene (on camera).

Lesson 4

In this lesson, pupils write a summary to finish off their review.

Introduction (10 mins)

It's time for the pupils to look over what they've written so far and get a sense of where it's all leading to – the final section! Invite certain children to read out their different sections to get a feel of how it flows together. You may want to get a group or two out to the front to read a section each to the rest of the class and invite feedback. How can we finish this off in a way that really brings this all together? What kind of things do we need for our conclusion?

Main (40 mins)

As a modelled write, demonstrate how to write a short summary to finish off your review, talking out loud as you go. Use the model example below if it helps, but talk the pupils through it so they can hear your thought processes as you go. Comment on how you are addressing the audience and choosing your vocabulary accordingly. For more able writers, discuss the use of the subjunctive (If I were...).

Example

I would give this book 5/5 stars! I learned that, sometimes, our imaginations can take us to amazing places. I think Max knew he had been naughty and rude to his mum, and that he wanted to escape into another world. If you have ever wanted to escape, then this is the book for you! If I were the author, I think I would have made sure that Max got into trouble on his adventure. If he had, maybe he would have learned his lesson.

As well as writing their summary, pupils also decide on the rating system your class will use, perhaps matching a theme in the book (for example, stars, marks out of ten, five thumbs up out of five...).

Partner children in similar-ability pairs. Pupils work with their partner to write a summary for the book review, choosing vocabulary to suit their audience. More able writers should be encouraged to use the subjunctive form. They also need to rate their book using the chosen system.

Plenary (20 mins)

Finally, start to put the writing you've been doing over the last four lessons into a sequence for the video. You can assign a section to each group of children and then give them time to edit their work and put their work into an order for the video. After they've had time to peer-edit and discuss an order, invite groups to share their sentences and give feedback.

Lesson 5

In this lesson, pupils decide on which sentences from Lesson 4 to include in the summary section, and the final few sequences are filmed, ready to put the finished video together. You should already have some work filmed from Lessons 1, 2 and 3, but before the lesson, choose extra sentences or paragraphs from the pupils' work to film today.

Introduction (15 mins)

Watch the example videos again (www.youtube.com/playlist?list=PL_odjZ7bN8F7e XHSM00lnY6ay7VD7B43Y) and discuss which features they would like to include in the final, collaborative video (for example, talking to camera, voice-over, action shots of people reading, etc.). Make a list of shots to be completed today. This could include:

- short video clips or images of children reading in the book corner or library
- photos of the book
- short video clips or stills of children holding up stars (or other rating)
- sentences or sections of text to include in the final video as voice-over or performed to camera
- acting out scenes from the book to go with voice-over sections.

Main (30 mins)

The filming can be done with each group filming their own video or you can assign different sections to different groups to make one collaborative video. Alternatively, if access to hardware is limited, you can invite groups up to the front of the class to record a section of their writing on camera whilst the rest of the class gives feedback on performances. Roles you can assign include:

- camera person
- director (silence, camera, action!)
- voice-over
- actors performing highlights
- pupils pretending to read.

Plenary (15 mins)

Review the footage you have so far as a whole class. If you have been filming and editing on the go using Adobe Spark Video, then you can edit and review as a whole class on the main board using your browser. This is a really fun experience and also models how to use Spark Video to your pupils. It also gives you the chance to re-record voice-overs if you need to.

To finish the project, you'll need to share the final book review with an audience. This could be by playing your video in a whole-school assembly, including it in your school newsletter or by publishing it online using your school's YouTube or Twitter account.

Chapter 10
STEM to STEAM

Introduction

STEM is more than just an acronym. Of course, it stands for Science, Technology, Engineering and Maths, but more than this, it represents a combination of these elements. It's greater than the sum of its parts. You hear the word STEM and you are immediately drawn to the fact-based, black or white, logic-resolved learning experiences, but bring in one simple letter 'A' and everything becomes a lot more STEAMy!

STEM is the mechanism which drives our increasingly complex world, in which rapidly advancing technology provides infinite possibilities for new applications of science, maths and engineering. But to take advantage of the myriad opportunities inherent in this complexity, we need something more than STEM. We need the Arts.

Enter STEAM: STEM with added creative energy, emotion and vision. This is the path to innovation.

In this chapter...

In this chapter we learn why the arts are a necessary addition to the world of STEM and why STEAM education is important. An interview with Dr Tim Fox, a Chartered Engineer and Fellow of the Institution of Mechanical Engineers, highlights what makes a great engineer and why, in schools, we should prioritise the skills needed for this role. The Atlas of the Future case study explores Little Inventors, an exciting initiative that invites children to share their ideas for inventions. Then turn to your own class of innovators to spend the day completing the LEGO™ WeDo Film For Flooding STEAM project.

The importance of STEAM

Science is the basis of human advancement. It is how we understand and explore our world. Through science, we ask questions about how things work and find answers to our problems. Sometimes we find answers to problems we hadn't even considered yet!

Science, enabled by maths, engineering and technology underpins our economy and our wellbeing. It drives our production of food, buildings, clothing and medicines. It's how we create safe drinking water, electricity and in fact, almost everything that we rely on every day.

Consider science and maths as 'the head' of STEAM, providing the reasoning needed to solve problems; contemplate engineering and technology as 'the body', enabling the practical application of the ideas developed with science and maths and see the arts as 'the heart', without which there would be no meaning or purpose and this is why STEAM is important.

Why the 'A'?

Our pupils need to have the STEM skills and drive to be the future problem solvers, but we also need them to be able to engage creatively, confidently, critically and collaboratively and this is where the arts come in.

STEM is all about exploring and solving problems. But the 'hard' skills of maths and science will only take us so far in this. It's not enough to know how to solve an equation. We also need to choose the right problems to solve.

It's not just about what we can do, but also about *why* we should do it. Because of their role in developing critical thinking skills, the arts and humanities have a huge role to play in this.

What's more, we need people in STEM to possess empathy, which is vital in understanding other perspectives. It enables us to see where the need for technological advancement really lies and to direct our efforts accordingly. It can make us more aware of the potential consequences of our scientific discoveries and of the technological advancements they make possible.

Training in the arts and humanities can help us to make sound ethical choices. History and philosophy, for example, support our understanding of who we want to be and where we want to go. Knowledge of these subjects can help us to be critical, not just of scientific procedures and findings, but of social systems and inequalities.

When we look carefully, we see that there are many natural overlaps or connections between the arts and STEM. As Dr Jenny Nash, Head of the Education Solutions Design Team at LEGO Education, says, 'A baker uses chemistry; a chemist develops the makeup and a computer animator designs the on-screen special effects used in the blockbuster movies we see in theatres. Experiencing STEAM subjects in an integrated way is more authentic and representative of the world we're preparing students to enter.'

Our pupils need to be ready for the ever-changing landscape of their futures. They need to be a future-ready workforce who understand the potential of 'what if' when solving problems in real life, to build a world that is better, safer and more equitable for humanity.

Talking point

What is a scientist? What does a scientist look like? Can you name a scientist?

Share with the class

In a study carried out in the 1960s and 1970s, boys and girls were asked to draw a picture of a scientist. The results revealed a stunning bias – 99.4 per cent of the drawings depicted a male scientist. Out of 5,000 drawings collected between 1966 and 1977, only 28 were of female scientists, all of which were drawn by girls (Edutopia, May 2019).

Since then, this experiment has been repeated in further studies with around 20,000 children from different age groups undertaking the activity. Pleasingly, the results have shown a significant increase in the children drawing the scientist as female. According to the latest meta-analysis, the average number of female scientists being drawn had risen to 28 per cent. Improved, but also still a concern (Edutopia, May 2019).

Programmes – such as the WISE Campaign, for example – have been set up to increase the number of women participating in STEM: www.wisecampaign.org.uk/about-us. However, far more still needs to be done to increase the engagement of those who are currently underrepresented. It's not just women who are under-represented: those from working-class backgrounds and some minority ethnic groups are also less likely to become involved in STEM.

The effect of this underrepresentation is a white washing of the sciences, both in the figurative and literal sense of the word. We are missing out on the nuanced, varied perspectives of entire social groups. This limits our thinking, perspective and ultimately, our ability to innovate. What we need is a workforce representative of all types of diversity, including cognitive diversity, to fully realise the potential benefits of STEAM in the future.

Why teach STEAM?

In simple terms – STEAM reflects real life!

Talking point

Describe a job or career that reflects the STEAM subjects. What career do you hope to follow? What aspects of a STEAM education, if any, would help you on this journey?

Jobs are multifaceted and interdisciplinary. We need to help children understand that subjects integrate and work together to resolve a problem. With STEAM, we can challenge preconceptions that learning is disparate. We can move on from the 'I'm good at maths and science, so I'm not creative' way of thinking.

We need to help children to develop diverse skills and to learn how to think critically and evaluate information, and also how to apply knowledge, research and skills to problem solve. We need to help them find a passion for growth and exploration and to be career-ready by enhancing their flexibility, adaptability, responsibility and innovation skills.

Providing a STEAM education where children 'learn through doing' prepares them for real life, as rarely are problems solved by abstract thought alone. A more experimental 'trial and error' approach provides much more depth to learning experiences. Children discover outcomes for themselves whether first time, or through making mistakes which confirm how not to do things, or through discovering previously unthought-of solutions. The added benefit of a practical and immersive learning approach is that it can stimulate learners of all styles. There's room within most practical situations to account for visual, auditory and kinaesthetic preferences.

Teaching STEAM doesn't mean ripping everything up and starting again. It does, however, mean refusing to be conventional. It means finding new ways of supporting children to be rounded thinkers, with skill sets that span both analytical and critical thinking. This union is the key to unlocking new perspectives, which is crucial if we are to confront the social and environmental challenges that we are certain to face in the coming decades.

We don't know where the future is going to take us. All that we can do is to equip generations to come with the rounded knowledge they need, in the hope that they will thrive, no matter what challenges they may face.

Interview with Tim Fox

Introducing...

Tim Fox is a Senior Fellow of the Institution of Mechanical Engineers (IMechE) – he sits on and chairs several of their senior boards. Tasked with thought leadership and investigating ideas, he is often their spokesperson on the TV and radio as well as giving talks all over the UK and overseas. His perspective on education and how it relates to engineering is absolutely fascinating because it gives a whole new perspective on the value of a rounded education.

What are the most important qualities of a successful engineer?

There are four things that I think make up a really great engineer. Firstly, of course they need to understand the first principles of engineering: the maths, physics and logical way of thinking that are at the core of engineering. Secondly, they are innovative.

They are looking for solutions that are genuinely different but remain rooted in the principles and practicalities of engineering. They are radical at the same time as being grounded. Thirdly, truly great engineers have an entrepreneurial streak – they understand the commercial obligations or drivers that underpin whatever they are looking to bring forward as an innovation. Finally, and perhaps not something that people often understand, they must be really good communicators. They understand how to communicate to different audiences, tailoring their message for the right occasion with good oracy and vocabulary skills. Funders, politicians and the general public all need a different message and the best engineers can do that.

So, when we're educating our future engineers, we need to get that mix right in order to give them the best possible set of skills for success. Typically, engineers are appalling communicators, very reticent and lacking in expressiveness, awareness and an understanding or empathy for the listener's needs and concerns. They haven't been taught those skills because they were streamed down the STEM path at an early age rather than perhaps a more arts-based route with more emphasis on communication skills.

Engineers are also generally terrible at understanding the social context for what they're doing and how their work fits within what's happening in the world. If you're going to create solutions for the biggest global problems facing society, like our Grand Challenges of the 21st century, you need some understanding of what things are important and why, empathy and engagement skills, and these are few and far between in the current crop of engineers.

Are there enough engineers and are they working on the right problems?

There's been a mantra about the shortage of engineers ever since I can remember, and though this is undoubtedly the case, the biggest challenge is to find good engineers capable of working effectively on society's most pressing problems. Lots of engineers are embedded in industries working solely to maintain the status quo and keep those businesses going, sustaining 'business-as-usual', and I wouldn't necessarily call that a good use of time compared to working on projects that actually matter for the future survival and wellbeing of the human race! But encouragingly there is a growing cohort of engineers who are more aware of society's fundamental challenges and want to do something about addressing them, which is in no small part thanks to the work of the IMechE in raising the profile of engineering and its potential to improve the world we live in.

How important is it for us to develop engineers?

The reality is that the challenges that we're facing in the 21st century are not going to be overcome without engineers. Everything that is contributing to those challenges was originally designed and put in place by engineers at a time when sustainability and greenhouse gas emissions reduction weren't on the agenda, society had consumption demands that needed to be met, and it was the role of an engineer to deliver. Back in the sixties for example, when the driving mantra for much of engineering was 'higher, faster, farther', the challenges were very different, but now we need to change and transition to more sustainable engineering solutions; solutions that still deliver economic development, but simultaneously tackle issues challenging our environment and ecosystems within a societal context (i.e. not harming society). For example, India is dealing with the struggle of delivering a development agenda to bring a large percentage of their population out of abject poverty at the same time as trying to ensure that it's done sustainably, so as not to cause problems further down the line. That all comes down to engineered systems, because with seven billion people on the planet fast approaching ten billion we're not going to get away with going back to becoming hunter gatherers, or to medieval times with everyone having a strip of land at the manor to farm on. The only plausible way forward is to transition our current systems sustainably using the best of engineering to do so. That is the challenge of our next generation of engineers.

What's your view of the current education system and how it attracts and educates future engineers?

To be blunt, it's not fit for purpose because we're not providing the correct balance of skills for engineers to practise engineering successfully in today's world. Students are getting streamed in secondary school and going down a purely science and maths route, which leaves them hugely capable of creating amazing technical solutions, but solutions that are often not commercially viable, not socially viable, or more disastrously, if they do meet those criteria they cannot communicate the potential of their solution to the right people.

Interestingly, a lot of people who would be disregarded as engineers by the traditional system can actually be the very people that we need, because it's not necessarily the academic we need; it's about motivation and insight. For example, I previously taught on a renewable energy engineering programme which was set up by the University of Exeter around 17 years ago. That programme took on students who hadn't been streamed into the STEM route at school, and actually in many cases couldn't stand maths and physics, but rather had come to the course with huge amounts of motivation for the problem they were trying to solve. That's so important because it created a passion which would push them through the hard slog of learning the basic principles of engineering, often taking them far beyond most of the more celebrated students in reaching workable plausible solutions. We're missing a huge swathe of potentially excellent engineers who don't feel like engineering is for them, or because they don't see engineering as part of the solution to the problem that they want to solve. But the interesting thing is that this totally different standpoint or starting point is exactly what makes them more likely to find a solution, because they're approaching it from a completely different perspective with a completely different level of motivation.

If you think about people who came into engineering in the fifties, sixties and seventies, they were turned on by supersonic aircraft, rockets, big oil refineries and nuclear power plants. They were turned on by the technology itself, just like I was with fighter jets and spacecraft, which drove them on to do the maths and the physics! The same motivation is there for people today, but now it's about environmental, sustainability and socially related problems, and they don't necessarily see engineering as a fundamental building block to help them realise their dream.

How should it be taught in schools?

Engineering needs to be embedded in everything, across the curriculum, providing people with windows into the world of engineering so that they can see it as a possible pathway for their passion. But crucially, we need to support those people who might not be naturally gifted at maths and science, because they are equally, if not more, important for the goal of finding the right solutions in the first place.

In the Exeter renewable energy engineering programme I mentioned earlier, I taught a ten-week maths foundation module set up for those who didn't have A-Level maths, to take them from the basics of first principles right the way through to advanced calculus, and those students would absolutely succeed. Interestingly, because they went through such effort to learn those basic principles, compared to the other students who had cruised through A-Level maths at school, some of those students made the best engineers and are now working successfully at the forefront in the renewables sector.

How would you use education to bring new solutions to market more quickly?

We need to educate young people to have the same relationship with, for example, the energy system as they currently have with their ICT, things like their tablets, smart watches and the iPhone. Individual products like solar panels aren't going to create the same emotional response as the iPhone, because the latter is a communication device, a human-to-human interaction providing communication on a mass scale. How do we get people to understand that energy is just as important to our wellbeing as communication? Most people don't think about their energy systems; they just walk in the room and turn the light on. You have to transition them somehow to have some affinity with it, and have some sense of ownership or stake in it, 'skin-in-the-game'.

I guess the closest we're getting at the moment is in how the EV market is marketing electric vehicles. For decades, we've had a strong marketing theme pushing the fossil-fuelled car as a means of projecting one's level of personal success to the outside world, and now we're trying to do it in the same way with EVs, trying to engender the same level of emotional response to an EV as to a petrol-guzzling Ford Mustang.

That's what will be so interesting about how home energy supply and use is evolving with powerwalls, or community energy projects, because they transform how people relate to energy: it's suddenly within their own personal realm. For example, if a big utility or out-of-town developer decides to put a wind turbine up at the end of my road, people will go nuts and NIMBY-ism will come out in force. But if the houses in my village all clubbed together to buy a wind turbine, and shared the power generated along with the profits from selling the excess, everyone's going to ask for two or three to be put up instead!

Education can socialise the market, so that sustainable solutions can be readily adopted or accepted as normal, and thereby prepare it for market entrants to engage. Starting with the big challenge, then introducing the systems that need to change, before showing them the individual products that will provide the solutions. It's about creating a coherent, engaging and plausible narrative which ends at the solution that you are proposing. This is 'socialising the market'.

Atlas of the Future case study: Little Inventors

Out of the mouths of babes… come wondrous ideas and fantastical plans. Ever seen a rucksack with wings? How about a fork that cools your food? Welcome to Little Inventors, where crayon drawings become real-life gadgets – inspiring a generation to keep believing that the only real limit is their imagination.

Kids have the enviable ability to look at the world like anything's possible, and Little Inventors makes sure that it is. They combine live invention workshops with an online idea gallery and a network of hands-on makers – to give children space to have ideas, show them to the world, and see them made real. It's the brainchild of Dominic Wilcox, the inventor behind the world's first GPS shoes, a tummy-rumble amplifier and a shelf made out of ivy – amongst many, many other wacky and wonderful things.

Keen to see what would happen when young minds were given free rein to create, he launched a series of workshops in his home town of Sunderland in 2015. 'The world has many problems and challenges,' he says, 'and we need to encourage more inventive thinkers to solve them.'

Dominic found an empty shop, and turned it into a gallery of inventive ideas. Over 450 children took part, and their designs were shown to a group of local artists. Five of them – a family scooter, a Liftolator (War Avoider), a shady lamp, a super fast tennis ball and a high-five machine – were made into prototypes that have since found a home in London's Victoria and Albert (V&A) Museum.

'I remember seeing the children's eyes light up when they saw their idea made real; it really makes them believe that their ideas are important and can lead to great things. We started to receive requests to do the same thing in other countries so we decided to start Little Inventors as a permanent project. Even at that very first Little Inventors event, I was really surprised at the standard of inventions. One little girl invented half a sleeping tablet where one side of your head went to sleep while the other half of your brain kept on working. The other one I remember was a little boy who invented a camera embedded in a tooth and whenever you smiled it took a photo.

At primary school, children's imaginations are very free and unrestricted. It's a magic period and a time when we can find really good ideas. The process is about getting them to look at challenges or entertaining ideas rather than being too serious or *Dragon's Den* style. Bonkers ideas are fine and the project is very much focused on flexing their creative muscle because if you don't keep using it, you can lose it. I think that's a problem with secondary education. Those kinds of ideas are not developed and that's a problem because problem-solving is a huge part of the creative process. When we don't exercise that muscle, we lose confidence in creative thinking. We must not fear failing. Some people can't cope with carrying an idea through so they protect themselves by not starting in order to protect themselves. Further down the line, this problem extends into the workplace.'

Now, kids can submit their ideas to the Little Inventors website, where a growing network of inventive grown-ups choose ideas they want to make real. These woodworkers, electrical engineers, costume makers, artists and roboticists – otherwise known as Magnificent Makers – document their making process and upload it via the Little Inventors blog, so young creators can see their idea come to life.

Recently, they teamed up with Ocado to launch the food waste challenge, asked children across the North of England to come up with future-facing ideas for the year 2030, and joined forces with Aquafresh to gather ideas to make tooth-brushing more fun. In 2017, Little Inventors made their way over to Canada, to bring STEAM learning to life in partnership with The Natural Sciences and Engineering Research Council of Canada (NSERC).

They have since partnered with the V&A Museum in London to connect kids to the Victorian spirit of invention. Exhibits made by little inventors can be found alongside the likes of Christopher Wren's drawings and Leonardo da Vinci's notebooks, and a free Little Inventors resource pack is available for teachers who want to inspire their pupils with the inventions of the past.

The team are now on the hunt for some next-level inventive energy in the form of Little Inventors Super Schools, which would get first access to the latest challenges and ideas and be linked to schools in other countries to work on invention ideas together.

Little Inventors is as much about bringing out imaginations as it is about reinforcing kids' belief that they can make solutions out of nothing. 'I've been amazed at the amount of enthusiasm people have for the project and the amount of children who have said "I want to be an inventor when I grow up!" after taking part.'

Most importantly, it's a platform for creating a culture of collaboration and practical possibilities. 'We believe that creativity is a great way to cross boundaries and create connections. We believe that anyone has the ability to be creative if they're given the chance, and that this open-minded thinking is important for creating a better future through all of us – through ingenious inventions, but also through helping people to work together.'

Discover more online: https://atlasofthefuture.org/project/little-inventors

Project 10: Film for flooding

Welcome to this full-day STEAM project. The aim is to create a working floodgate using LEGO WeDo that will help to control the negative effects of flooding through excess rainfall. As well as creating a model, pupils will record their progress using a camera and use it to put together an Adobe Spark Video which communicates their work to an audience.

Teaching tip

This project assumes that your pupils are familiar with building and programming LEGO WeDo using the app. Also, make sure you have Adobe Spark Video installed on your devices and an account that your class can use later in the challenge. If this is your first time using WeDo, you can get your class up to speed by doing some of the following models in the WeDo app:

- glowing snail
- cooling fan
- moving satellite.

They are pretty quick to complete but importantly they get children programming their creations and using sensors. The WeDo app has all the building instructions you need and you can also use the app's programme library in order to work out how to use the coding blocks.

Morning session

The morning session is all about getting hands on with the equipment, learning how to use the LEGO WeDo app, working as a team and each group documenting their progress by taking photos for use in the afternoon session.

Introduction (30 mins)

Explain to pupils that today they are going to create a working floodgate using LEGO WeDo that will help to control the negative effects of flooding through excess rainfall. In preparation, discuss what your class knows about flooding. Write notes on the board for later use.

- What is flooding?
- How does it happen?
- Has anyone ever been affected by flooding?
- What damage can it cause?
- Are there any long-term effects?

Next, watch videos on flooding to help give context to the problem your pupils will be solving.

- Floods bring 'danger to life' as heavy rain batters UK – ITV News: www. youtube.com/watch?v=lGTsiNjBiww
- Storm Jorge brings further destructions to the UK: www.youtube.com/ watch?v=L6tsJgI7wtg
- Venice is flooded by the highest tides since 1960s: www.youtube.com/ watch?v=4BKk84P8Ih4

Now that they have seen some more information on flooding, ask them if there's anything they want to add to the notes on the board. Finally, look at floodgates and their different scales.

- Residential floodgates: Google 'front door residential floodgates' and look at the image results.
- River floodgates: Google 'river floodgates' and look at the image results.
- Huge dams: Google 'river dams' and look at the image results.

Planning (20 mins)

Split your class into groups who will work together with a WeDo kit. Ask pupils to work in their groups to plan their floodgate model by completing the STEAM Design Brief worksheet, available in the online resources.

Teaching tip

For the third section of the worksheet, it might be useful to look for support in the guided projects section of the LEGO WeDo app which has a prevent flooding guided project with useful information.

Building (40 mins)

Give groups time to build their floodgates and play around with the coding controls. Tell groups that during this time it will be useful if they take regular photos of what is happening so that they can use the images to create their video at the end of the project.

Testing (20 mins)

Ask each group to share some of the insights they got from their building phase as they demo to the rest of the class how their prototype works. Every time an insight is shared, generate some discussion and develop the class's understanding further. This might be relating to:

- how flooding might be tackled using a floodgate
- ways of coding their creation to do various tasks
- sensors: they might be both inputs and outputs (warning lights and sounds, motion sensors triggering the floodgate to close, etc.).

Make notes on the board of the most insightful discussions, questions and statements from the class. These will be useful in the final stage of the project when they put together an Adobe Spark Video of their progress and insights.

Video planning (30 mins)

Now, get each group to plan their Adobe Spark Video, which communicates what they have been doing, using the Spark Video Template. You can watch an example video of what your groups are going to create here: www.youtube.com/watch?v=sLJkWPomAR0

The following steps will form the structure of the video. Go through each step as a whole class using the notes that you have taken so far:

- Step 1 – Introduction: Who are you? Where are you from? What have you been researching?

- Step 2 – The big problem: What problem are you trying to solve? Why is it happening?

- Step 3 – Your invention: What does your invention do? Describe a situation where it could help.

- Step 4 – The detail: How does your invention work? What sensors have you used?

Add to the notes you've made as you discuss appropriate responses to each step so that the class has detailed notes that they can refer to for guidance when filming their videos. Allow time for each group to write their steps.

Teaching tip

You might want to assign a group member as the person in charge of each step so that they can work on making the writing for one step the best that it can be.

Afternoon session

This session is all about pupils presenting their learning in a format which allows other people to see what they have learned, their thought processes and conclusions as well as how they went about creating their models.

Filming introduction (20 mins)

Revisit the example video of what your groups are going to create using Adobe Spark Video and their Spark Video Template. I recommend that you allow your groups to film Step 1 as a video but then encourage voice-overs to be used for Steps 2–4, using photos taken during the build session or video footage that they record to match the voice-over.

Prepare the class by talking to them about:

- steady camera work
- recording voice-overs
- clear speech
- making the visuals match the audio.

Filming (10 mins)

Give your groups 15 minutes to film Step 1 of their plan. Tell them that rather than doing it as one continuous shot, break it down into one sentence per shot to keep it nice and snappy. Encourage them to self-assign roles and swap over for each step. The roles could be:

- director (the person who wrote that step)
- tablet or recording device operator
- actors, one per sentence.

Editing (30 mins)

Once the first step has been filmed, give groups time to record voice-overs for steps 2–4. Encourage them to self-assign roles and swap over for each step:

- director (the person who wrote that step)
- tablet or recording device operator
- voice-over artists, one per sentence.

Teaching tip

Use your large screen to show how to edit sound, add text and icons if necessary, use split screen layouts and finally to add music.

Showcase (30 minutes)

Once the editing is complete, use your large screen to showcase the videos made by each group.

- If you are all logged into one Spark Video account, then you can easily do this by selecting the right video from the My Videos list.
- If each group has a unique account, then get them to use the SHARE button to send you their link using email or Google Classrooms.

Take feedback from the class for each video. Celebrate the positives and suggest edits for improvements.

Final words

Writing this book has been an education to me thanks in no small part to the army of interviewees I pestered for insights over the course of a year. Many are featured in this book but others can be found on the website accompanying this book, and I would urge you to check them out. It is with great regret that not all of them made it to print, but this book would have been impossible to carry if they had! As a class teacher, I have often found it easy to fall into the trap of being the authority on what works in the classroom. Thankfully, the wisdom and experience of all the interviewees opened my eyes to a world of insights from other perspectives, many of which had never occurred to me.

It was the effervescent Michael Rosen, with whom I have had the pleasure of working for a few years, who gave one of the simplest and yet most profound points on how we don't teach children about the future. Most of the work on this book happened before COVID-19 and school closures, but this challenging moment in history has brought Michael's point home even more than I expected.

I have been challenged many times for addressing issues of the environment and politics with younger children in the classroom but it seems to me crazy that exploring ideas around the future, our human relationships as an exponentially increasingly population and our stewardship of this wonderful planet, with those young people who will bear the brunt of our short-sightedness as adults should be avoided. In the words of Cathy Runciman from Atlas of the Future in her interview in Chapter 5, encouraging people to take part in shaping a fairer and more sustainable future that will truly benefit everyone, everywhere, seems to me to be the most important role that teachers have.

The future is bright as long as we put it in the hands of an eyes-wide-open generation of children. Teachers play a huge role in that mission and my hope is that this book will empower us all to play our part in bringing hope, joy, optimism and purpose into our classrooms.

With that in mind, I would like to leave you with one final interview, with the excellent Lord Jim Knight, who joins me in calling for this positive disruption in schools.

Dominic Traynor

Interview with Lord Jim Knight

Introducing...

Jim Knight is Chief Education Adviser at TES Global. He was Labour's longest-serving Schools Minister in the previous Labour government and also served as Rural Affairs Minister and Employment Minister. Jim's main policy interests are education, employment, skills, rural affairs and digital technology. He is a member of the House of Lords and a visiting professor at the London Knowledge Lab of the Institute of Education.

You're quite outspoken on schools being unfit for purpose. Can you go into detail about why you think that?

The commercial organisations that I talk to and observe, the ones that are successful, are the ones that are getting into investing and learning. They're investing in the talents that they have in their own organisations. They also frequently complain that they have a shortage of talent. Ernst & Young, Google and AXA have all talked about how they're not so interested in students going to university because they'd rather train those young people themselves and teach them the skills that they want them to develop, which schools and universities aren't teaching. In this fourth industrial age, that all leads to talking about how we can't just train young people to compete with machines, which is largely what is happening in schools. The easiest way to think about that is: what is the competitive advantage of humans over future machines? For me, it is about developing the uniquely human skills, which are empathy and our ability to improvise and think laterally across disciplines.

Todd Rose's book, *The End of Average*, opens with a great anecdote around when fast jets were first used in the US Air Force. They had a very high crash rate and it was blamed on pilot error, but in the end, it turned out it was because cockpits were designed around an average size specification for pilots, and as a result, they didn't have adjustable seats. So, we now have adjustable seats in cars as a result of that insight. That's the kind of thing humans can do that machines can't.

Then you have the other well-known things starting with 'c': creativity, communication, collaboration... There is so much around collaboration and yet we have a whole education system that is about individual performance and individual assessments. I can't conceive of any job where you are not going to be required to collaborate with other humans and machines.

What is the point of school?

There are many reasons why I think parents want their kids to go to school, not least because society requires kids to go to school. Once, learners themselves enjoyed getting up in the morning and wanted to go to school. We are born learning naturally; that's what we do and we get great satisfaction out of learning. The unfortunate reality for too many young people is that school is a place where you have a rest from learning. A large part of the problem is that, right now, we desperately need innovative, entrepreneurial, disruptive, valued creators but this doesn't quite fit with any of our current schooling models. We're far more focused on keeping the status quo than fostering positive disruption and that is a problem for society at large.

What is your opinion of the current curriculum?

I think we teach a lot of things that don't matter very much. Where I'd like to get to with the curriculum begins with a 0-7-years-old phase that is very much about socialisation, learning from each other on a day-to-day basis and mostly learning through play and through solving problems. That's very much learning from what works in Scandinavia. In particular, this would be more for boys because there's research that suggests that forcing boys to sit still when they are about four or five will turn them off school forever. Then, I would enter the 7-14 phase, ending the National Curriculum at 14, which is much more about a broad and balanced curriculum and the framework of knowledge and understanding, making sure the core skills of reading and writing, and numeracy and computational thinking, are there. And I would add that historical narratives are important to understand your place in the world and the shape of civilisation.

Finally, we then enter the last phase. 14-19 years old is when young people have a really good spread of time to engage in collaborative learning, problem-based learning and different styles of learning to really understand where their interests lie in the labour market. We're talking four years to really explore your talents, and explore what makes you want to get up in the morning, and what you really love and what your superpowers are. But it's so important to develop that positive attitude to learning because the rest of their lives will be all about working and learning and changing careers multiple times, which means that universities can develop a much longer business model than they currently do by unbundling their programmes and making learning part of a much more ongoing, bite-size model that allows students to adapt to the job market and their own desires.

In terms of how that would affect schools, I spoke to a headteacher who made the excellent point that we should be making young people sit the minimum number of exams to get to the next stage – so five GCSEs is enough for them to do A levels, and then they should do A levels efficiently enough to get into university if that's the journey they want to take. If you take it down to five GCSEs, what a lot of time and money you will have saved to do whatever learning you care to do. Now, there will be some people saying, 'Give me more physics; give me more chemistry', so take them down that path. Others might say, 'I love maths! Give me pure maths, give me additional maths, give me applied maths, give me all the maths!' But not everyone wants to do maths and cutting down on GCSEs allows young people to find their passions or at least their strong points.

I fundamentally believe in individual talents and our job is to bring that out. I have a belief that everyone has a genius, and I have a belief that we waste most of it because we never discover it. Now we have the opportunity to be something close to immortal to some extent and we have some very serious questions to ask whether or not we want that. Our progress has come about at the expense of the environment, community and mental health. Less war, less famine, more luxuries and yet we're more stressed and unhappy. It would be silly to say that is just an effect of social media. It's a conflation of many things but school is the universal service for children. It's time to think about the school system as a whole and what role the school system has in making childhood better.

References

Introduction

www.thejournal.ie/smoking-in-schools-1831499-Jan2015

https://edition.cnn.com/2018/03/23/world/plastic-great-pacific-garbage-patch-intl/index.html

www.ladbible.com/trashisles/welcome

https://olioex.com/food-waste/the-problem-of-food-waste

https://publications.parliament.uk/pa/cm201719/cmselect/cmenvaud/1491/149105.htm

www.theguardian.com/environment/2017/oct/24/uk-30-40-years-away-eradication-soil-fertility-warns-michael-gove

www.bbc.co.uk/news/health-34932478

www.centreformentalhealth.org.uk/blog/centre-mental-health-blog/children-new-century-mental-health-11-year-olds

Chapter 1

http://www.ukya.org.uk/why-dont-young-people-vote/

https://www.economist.com/britain/2018/02/03/the-myth-of-the-youthquake-of-2017

https://www.theguardian.com/news/2018/nov/29/why-we-stopped-trusting-elites-the-new-populism

https://www.theguardian.com/environment/2018/dec/04/leaders-like-children-school-strike-founder-greta-thunberg-tells-un-climate-summit

https://www.telegraph.co.uk/women/politics/michelle-obama-12-things-know-went-london-talk/

https://eu-rope.ideasoneurope.eu/2017/11/14/fake-news-caused-brexit/

Chapter 2

Abarca-Gómez, L., Abdeen, Z. A., Hamid, Z. A., et al. (2017), 'Worldwide trends in body-mass index, underweight, overweight, and obesity from 1975 to 2016: a pooled analysis of 2416 population-based measurement studies in 128.9 million children, adolescents, and adults', *The Lancet*, 390(10113), 2627–2642.

Adab, P., Pallan, M. J., Lancashire, E. R., et al. (2018), 'Effectiveness of a childhood obesity prevention programme delivered through schools, targeting 6 and 7 year olds: cluster randomised controlled trial (WAVES study)', *British Medical Journal*, 360, k211.

Darbre, P. D. (2017), 'Endocrine disruptors and obesity', *Current Obesity Reports*, 6(1), 18–27.

Hurst, D. (2018), 'How Amsterdam is reducing child obesity.' News article available at: https://www.bbc.co.uk/news/health-43113760

Kim, P., Evans, G. W., Chen, E., et al. (2018), 'How Socioeconomic Disadvantages Get Under the Skin and into the Brain to Influence Health Development Across the Lifespan', in: Halfon, N., Forrest, C., Lerner, R., Faustman, E. (eds), *Handbook of Life Course Health Development*. Springer.

Monbiot, G. (2018), 'We're in a new age of obesity. How did it happen? You'd be surprised.' News article available at: https://www.theguardian.com/commentisfree/2018/aug/15/age-of-obesity-shaming-overweight-people

OECD (2017), 'Health at a glance 2017: OECD Indicators.' OECD Publishing. http://dx.doi.org/10.1787/health_glance-2017-en

Ponterio, E. and Gnessi, L. (2015), 'Adenovirus 36 and obesity: An overview', *Viruses*, 7(7), 3719–40. doi:10.3390/v7072787

RCPCH (Undated), 'About childhood obesity.' Available at: https://www.rcpch.ac.uk/key-topics/nutrition-obesity/about-childhood-obesity

Schwartz, B. S., Pollak, J., Bailey-Davis, L., et al. (2015), 'Antibiotic use and childhood body mass index trajectory', *International Journal Of Obesity*, 40, 615.

WHO (2018), 'Taking action on childhood obesity.' Available at https://www.who.int/end-childhood-obesity/publications/taking-action-childhood-obesity-report/en/

Wilks, D. C., Sharp, S. J., Ekelund, U., et al. (2011), 'Objectively measured physical activity and fat mass in children: a bias-adjusted meta-analysis of prospective studies', *PloS one*, 6(2), e17205. doi:10.1371/journal.pone.0017205

Chapter 4

https://www.legofoundation.com/media/1063/learning-through-play_web.pdf

http://www.playengland.net/wp-content/uploads/2015/09/play-for-a-change-low-res.pdf

http://www.importanceofplay.eu/IMG/pdf/dr_david_whitebread_-_the_importance_of_play.pdf

https://www.teachers.org.uk/education-policies/primary/crisis-in-primary-assessment

https://www.tes.com/news/horror-show-it-difficult-comprehend-governments-stupidity-over-testing-schools

https://theconversation.com/stressed-out-the-psychological-effects-of-tests-on-primary-school-children-58913

https://www.theguardian.com/education/2016/may/01/parents-to-keep-children-out-of-school-in-key-stage-exam-boycott

http://pediatrics.aappublications.org/content/119/1/182

Coolahan, K., Fantuzzo J., Mendez J., McDermott, P. (2000), 'Preschool peer interactions and readiness to learn: relationships between classroom peer play and learning behaviors and conduct', *Journal of Educational Psychology*, 92, 458–465

Office of the United Nations High Commissioner for Human Rights, 'Convention on the Rights of the Child. General Assembly Resolution 44/25 of 20 November 1989'. Available at: www.unhchr.ch/html/menu3/b/k2crc.htm. Accessed June 22, 2006

Chapter 5

https://www.1843magazine.com/technology/rewind/the-true-history-of-fake-news (1843 Magazine, June 2017)

https://www.npr.org/2018/08/22/640883503/long-before-facebook-the-kgb-spread-fake-news-about-aids (NPR, August 2018)

https://infolit.org.uk/the-role-of-information-literacy-in-the-fight-against-fake-news/ (Information Literacy Group, February 2018)

https://www.commonsensemedia.org/sites/default/files/uploads/research/census_research report.pdf (Common Sense Media, 2015)

https://edexec.co.uk/schools-must-work-harder-to-combat-the-impact-of-fake-news/ (Education Executive, 2018)

https://www.bbc.co.uk/news/education-44454844 (BBC, June 2018)

https://oecdeducationtoday.blogspot.com/2017/12/educating-our-youth-to-care-about-each.html (Andreas Schleicher, December 2017)

https://www.independent.co.uk/news/uk/home-news/school-children-taught-recognise-fake-news-donald-trump-andreas-schleicher-a7636251.html (*Independent*, March 2017)

http://time.com/5505441/mark-zuckerberg-mentor-facebook-downfall/ (*Time Magazine*, January 2019)

Chapter 6

Baden, D. (2018), 'Environmental storytelling can help spread big ideas for saving the planet', *The Conversation*. Available at: https://theconversation.com/environmental-storytelling-can-help-spread-big-ideas-for-saving-the-planet-107621

Bar-On, Y. M., Philips, R., Milo, R. (2018), 'The biomass distribution on Earth', *Proceedings of the National Academy of Sciences*, 115(25) https://doi.org/10.1073/pnas.1711842115

Ceballos, G., Ehrlich, P. R., Dirzo, R. (2017), 'Population losses and the sixth mass extinction', *Proceedings of the National Academy of Sciences*, 114(30) https://doi.org/10.1073/pnas.1704949114

'Convention on Biological Diversity About Climate Change and Biological Diversity' (undated). Available at: https://www.cbd.int/climate/intro.shtml

Johnson, M. D., Kellermann, J. L., Stercho, A. M. (2010), 'Pest reduction services by birds in shade and sun coffee in Jamaica', *Animal Conservation*, 13, 140–147.

Press, C. (2018), 'Passing the baton: will young people take up the fight to save the planet?', *Guardian*. Available at: https://www.theguardian.com/australia-news/2018/sep/29/passing-the-baton-will-young-people-take-up-the-fight-to-save-the-planet

https://ourworld.unu.edu/en/world-environment-day-can-technology-save-us

Chapter 7

https://www.bbc.co.uk/news/uk-46347767

https://www.theguardian.com/education/2014/jul/29/chilld-and-adolescent-mental-health-service-failing-children

https://www.theguardian.com/society/2018/nov/22/what-is-happening-with-childrens-mental-health

https://www.theguardian.com/society/2018/aug/31/calls-for-action-over-uks-intolerable-child-mental-health-crisis

https://www.independent.co.uk/news/health/mental-health-children-nhs-england-depression-anxiety-report-young-people-a8646211.html

https://www.theguardian.com/society/2017/dec/03/children-with-mental-health-issues-to-get-more-help-but-not-until-the-2020s

Chapter 8

'UK throwing away £13bn worth of food each year, latest figures show', *Guardian*, January 2017. Available at: https://www.theguardian.com/environment/2017/jan/10/uk-throwing-away-13bn-of-food-each-year-latest-figures-show

Willersinn, C., Mack, G., Mouron, P., et al. (2015), 'Quality and quantity of food losses along the Swiss potato supply chain: Stepwise investigation and the influence of quality standards on losses', *Waste Management*, 46, 120–132.

'Half of all US food produce is thrown away, new research suggests', *Guardian*, July 2016. Available at: https://www.theguardian.com/environment/2016/jul/13/us-food-waste-ugly-fruit-vegetables-perfect

'No time for leftovers: The astonishing scale of food waste in the UK and around the world', *Telegraph*, January 2018. Available at: https://www.telegraph.co.uk/news/2018/01/02/no-time-leftovers-astonishing-scale-food-waste-uk-around-world

'Charity calls for £15m fund to tackle UK hunger by preventing food waste', *Guardian*, March 2018. Available at: https://www.theguardian.com/environment/2018/mar/28/charity-calls-for-15m-fund-to-tackle-uk-hunger-by-preventing-food-waste

'Food insecurity: a third of poorest households skip meals, survey finds', *Guardian*, January 2018. Available at: https://www.theguardian.com/global-development/2018/jan/30/food-insecurity-a-third-of-poorest-households-skip-meals-survey-finds

Ranganathan, J., Waite, R., Searchinger, T. and Hanson, C. (2018), 'How to sustainably feed 10 billion people by 2050, in 21 charts'. WRI. Available at: https://www.wri.org/blog/2018/12/how-sustainably-feed-10-billion-people-2050-21-charts

Chapter 9

https://theharrispoll.com/lego-group-kicks-off-global-program-to-inspire-the-next-generation-of-space-explorers-as-nasa-celebrates-50-years-of-moon-landing/

Chapter 10

https://www.edutopia.org/article/50-years-children-drawing-scientists

Index